# A Year in Tōkyō

an illustrated guide & memoir of 13 magical months
spent exploring the city of ginkgo leaves

### Christy Anne Jones

## *Follow*

  christyannejones.com

  YouTube.com/c/aileaux

  @christyannejones

Copyright © Christy Anne Jones 2022

All rights reserved. No part of this publication may be reproduced, stored in a retrieval system, or transmitted, in any form, or by any means (electronic, mechanical, photocopying, recording or otherwise) without the prior written permission of the author.

# Foreword

The summer after I turned 21, I moved to Tōkyō.

The moment my boyfriend, Tyler, and I stepped off of the plane, we were plunged into the humidity of the Japanese summer. We had no jobs, no long term accommodation and only spoke some conversational Japanese.

On that sticky July evening, we cleared customs, found our suitcases, and dragged them into the immigration office at Narita Airport. Less than half an hour later, we were each handed our *zairyū* cards—the physical markers of our new-found residence that we, as foreigners, would have to keep on us at all times. We left that little office, with its grey walls and carpet, its dim lighting, piles of paperwork and whirring fax machines, and officially started one of the most challenging and surreal adventures of our lives.

This illustrated guide and memoir is a curated collection of my very favourite moments from living in Japan. Here you will find snippets of great happiness and great anxiety; recommendations of my favourite things to do; guides to festival activities and local food; anecdotes about daily life; bits of folklore and culture; and, of course, tips and tricks for travel.

More so, this little book contains my own journey: a realistic, unembellished look at what it was like to live in the world's biggest city—how I grew, how I changed and what I learned. I have gained so very much from the thirteen months I spent living in Japan, and I am so excited to share it with you.

I hope you enjoy your journey through the city of ginkgo leaves.

# Table of Contents

- 5. Map
- 6. Why Tōkyō?
- 8. About Tōkyō

### 10. Summer
- 18. Summer Survival Tips
- 20. Ikebukuro
- 23. Train Etiquette
- 24. Shinjuku
- 25. Art & Stationery Shop Guide
- 26. Shibuya
- 28. Harajuku
- 33. Tōkyō Health Food Store Guide
- 34. Omotesandō

### 38. Autumn
- 44. Kichijōji
- 46. Mitaka
- 47. Ghibli Museum
- 50. Jimbōchō
- 54. Halloween in Japan
- 56. Tōkyō Disneyland
- 60. Mount Takao

### 64. Winter
- 66. Ueno
- 67. Museum Guide
- 70. Bookshop Guide
- 74. Odaiba
- 76. Yokohama

- 78. Christmas in Japan
- 80. Nakameguro
- 83. Cheap Restaurant Guide
- 86. Snow
- 89. J-Dramas to Binge Watch

### 90. Spring
- 92. Sangenjaya
- 97. Where to See Sakura
- 99. How to Hanami
- 100. Shimokitazawa
- 104. Tōkyō Station Area
- 106. Asakusa
- 108. Kamakura
- 110. Enoshima

### 112. Summer Again
- 115. Sayama Hills
- 116. Summer Reading List
- 117. Shinjuku Gyoen Garden
- 118. Odawara
- 119. Hakone
- 123. Onsen How-To
- 124. Matsuri Season
- 126. Tanabata

- 134. Life as an Ex-expat
- 136. P.S.
- 138. 7 Day Tōkyō Itinerary
- 140. Index

*Introduction*

# Why Tōkyō?

I've been (loosely) studying the Japanese language and culture since I was five years old. I remember watching the television special *Big Bird in Japan* during my Japanese class in Year One, enamoured by the plastic food displays and cluttered streets; I studied the language throughout high school and university and, when I was 19, after a lot of saving, went on my first trip.

Tōkyō was the first foreign city I ever visited. It was the first place I ever ran away to. No matter how many beautiful cities I've visited since, I will never recreate what it felt like to walk through Shinjuku for the very first time.

I fell in love with this bright, bustling city and its meticulously clean neighbourhoods and neon lights and sweet leafy suburbs tucked between it all. I fell in love with details: the vibrant changing seasons, the sharp chimes of the traffic lights, the stray cats padding across stone walls, and the illustrations on the soymilk packaging.

*Introduction*

Japan is a flawed, nuanced, normal place just like any other country in the world. Both hyper idealisation and stereotypical perceptions of 'weirdness' come from cultural bias.

But even still, as a person who had grown up her entire life in country and suburban South Australia, it was remarkable to be somewhere so different.

I was uncomfortable and learning every single second, and I loved it.

My boyfriend and I had worked relentlessly to save for that first holiday but, from that moment in Shinjuku, neither of us could get Tōkyō out of our heads. So, when I graduated from my Bachelor's, I made the choice to take up my post grad studies with a university that offered an online pathway. Tyler, also a student, did the same. From there, we began our planning.

We spent months researching visas, culture, work pathways and neighbourhoods to live in. It didn't for a second feel real. I grew up in a tiny town of less than 500 people, next to dairy cows and tractors.

How could I possibly be moving to the world's biggest city?

And yet, that's where we found ourselves: in Tōkyō, in sweltering July, with no jobs, no tickets home, holding our Working Holiday Visas in hand.

# About Tōkyō

Tōkyō is the world's biggest city. It's home to an estimated 13.5 million people (11% of Japan's total population), and stretches over 2,191 square kilometres.

Within this guide, we will be spending most of our time in the 23 special wards of Tōkyō; these wards, or neighbourhoods, include Shinjuku, Shibuya, Shinagawa, Itabashi and more.

23 Special Wards

Within these 23 special wards are smaller cities. For example, Shinjuku (itself) is a busy city within Shinjuku Ward. Nishidai, where our first apartment was located, is in Itabashi Ward. Ikebukuro is in Toshima Ward. Shibuya, Harajuku and our second apartment in Tōkyō are all located in Shibuya Ward.

*Introduction*

Tōkyō might be the world's biggest city, but it's one of the safest and most comfortable places I've ever visited. There's a lot of English signage, amenities like *konbini* (convenience stores) and vending machines are abundant with affordable food and drink options, and although Tōkyō has crime like any other city, theft is so low people leave their bags unattended on food court tables to reserve seating.

peach-flavoured water from the vending machine ↙

Despite the complexity of Tōkyō's layout, and the many definitions of what 'Tōkyō' actually is (Tōkyō Metropolis, Tōkyō Prefecture and Tōkyō Station area are all different), it's much less overwhelming once you get there.

*Tip:* if you're travelling to Tōkyō and you find the subway confusing, you can always default to the Yamanote Line. This is a loop line that'll take you to most of the major hubs of the city before circling back on itself.

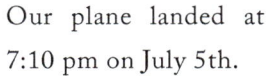

Our plane landed at 7:10 pm on July 5th.

The months prior had been a nerve-wracking blur of stress and activity: quitting our retail jobs, starting online university, and flying from Adelaide to Melbourne to pick up our visas from the closest Japanese Embassy.

We'd said goodbye to our loved ones at 5 am in the departures lounge of Adelaide Airport, and flew eleven hours to a different hemisphere. We had one goal: to last at least six months.

The first night was a wash of stress and overwhelming heat. An hour bus ride from Narita Airport. Clinging to huge suitcases in a rush hour train. A tiny hotel room in Ikebukuro, northern Tōkyō, with a piddly air conditioner. A *konbini* dinner of carbonara and curry.

The next morning, we dragged our suitcases onto the subway again, and travelled yet further north from Ikebukuro along the Tōbu Tōjō Line. The heat of the asphalt burnt Tyler's suitcase wheels right off.

Eventually, we found ourselves in an old weatherboard apartment in Nishidai, signing a contract on an iPad with sweaty hands. The realtors left us to the cicadas, and to slowly discover the mould and cannisters of cockroach bait.

But we finally caught our breath. We officially lived in Tōkyō.

*Life in Tōkyō*

# Our First Apartment

the view from our window →

our Nishidai apartment

Our first apartment was in Nishidai, Itabashi Ward—one of the northernmost wards of Tōkyō. Nishidai Station was a fifteen-minute walk to the north of our place; Tōbu-Nerima Station was twenty-two minutes south.

Here in the north, rent is considerably cheaper than in central Tōkyō. While our previous holidays in Japan had made us most familiar with the popular western wards of Shibuya and Shinjuku, we wanted to start out by exploring areas we had never visited before. The neighbourhood was quiet, filled mostly with elderly people and families, and we rarely saw any other foreigners.

*Life in Tōkyō*

For people with short-term visas, housing can be tricky.

Our Working Holiday Visas were approved in six-month bursts. This meant that we were ineligible for the normal two-year rentals that most people have in Japan.

And so, we decided to organise everything before leaving Australia; we went online, found a short-term apartment and booked it.

These 'foreigner friendly' apartments are a lot more expensive month-to-month than normal housing. However, the real estate agents speak English, and you're able to bypass a number of inconveniences such as paying the pricey upfront moving fees that are required in Japan, needing a guarantor signature and the fact that not all Japanese landlords are willing to rent to foreigners.

Unlike in Australia, the rent of a Japanese apartment is significantly impacted by how far it is from the train station. In my home country, most people drive. In Tōkyō, however, cars are a luxury, and most people get to work by train.

Of the short-stay options available, our apartment was cheap: ¥50,580 per month for our teeny-tiny space in a very old building, with a small separate kitchen and a tiny, plastic bathroom.

The washing machine was outside, covered in dirt and shared by the whole complex. We were too intimidated by it; for that month, we washed our clothes in the bath.

window sill cicada →

 *Life in Tōkyō*

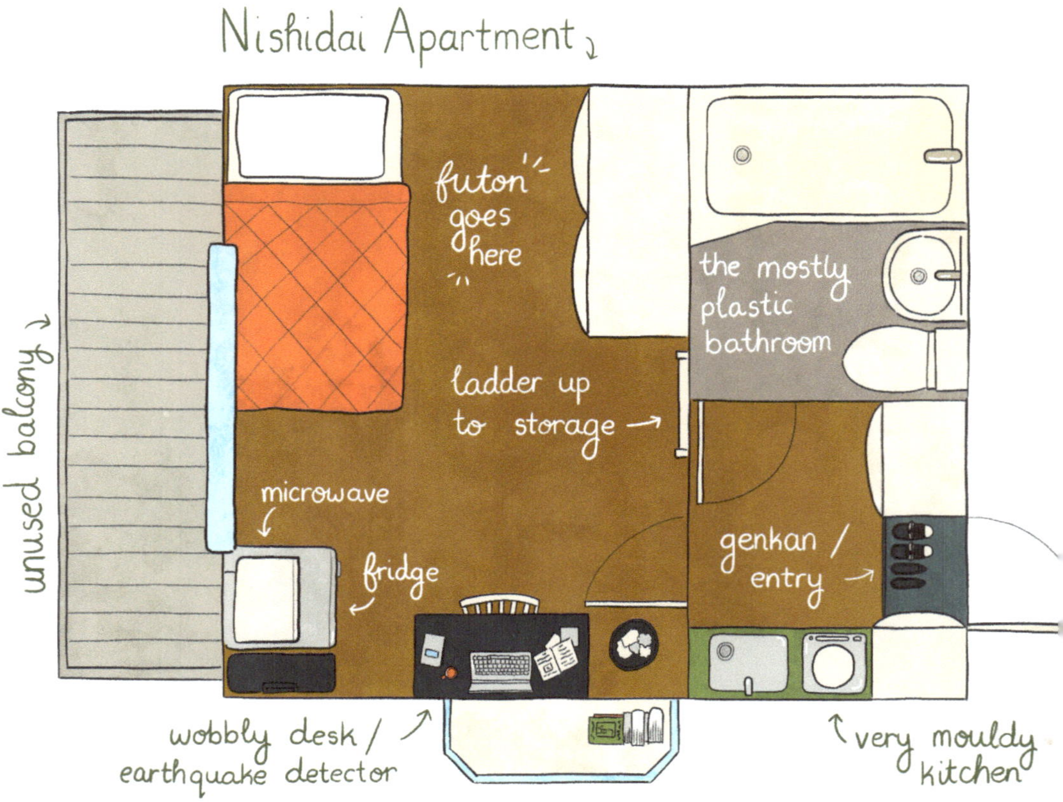

The apartment was a 17 square metre '1K' (one room, a separate kitchen, and a bathroom). Mould was splattered across the windowsills and kitchen, which we tried and **failed** to scrub away with mould cleaner.

We'd realised a little too late in the booking process that there was only one single bed in the apartment. The photos had been taken with a fish-eye lens to make the space seem bigger, so we hadn't realised the bed wasn't a double.

But they gave us a *futon* for the floor, and we made do. The mouldy kitchen went mostly unused—we lived off of microwave *gyōza*, ¥290 spaghetti and ice cream from the convenience store down the hill. Without a kettle or teaspoons, I made green tea in the microwave and mixed it with a plastic chopstick.

*Life in Tōkyō*

The first week passed quickly, and during the second we experienced our first earthquake. I woke at 2 am to the whole building shaking. The next night, I sat at our rickety desk editing a script for my screen writing class, when the wobbles alerted me that another small one had begun.

our neighbour's vegetable garden →

taken from our balcony on a rainy day ←

We were so frugal with money at this time that we barely even used the air conditioner. But, our second week ended, and I received a life changing email. I had been offered to interview for a paid internship! With the arrival of that news, I became hopeful that our fears of going home early would soon disappear.

It was a dream role, working with an artist who I had spent years admiring. I had applied for the internship before we had even left Australia, and now I was scheduled to interview in a trendy suburb, over an hour away in central Tōkyō. I wore the pink shirt that I had bought for my university graduation, and tried not to sweat on it as I walked to the train station, nervous and excited.

*Life in Tōkyō*

# To the grocery store

eggs
卵

soy milk

gyōza

bananas
バナナ

microwave spaghetti

croquettes
コロッケ

spring onion
ネギ

*Life in Tōkyō*

What struck me the most in those first weeks was how tiny differences could be so impactful. We couldn't, for example, find oats; this ruled out porridge for breakfast and our fear of the kitchen made pancakes out of the question. We had no toaster. I'm not a fan of cereal. And so, out of options, I settled on microwave, frozen *onigiri* (triangular balls of rice) for breakfast. No, this wasn't terribly nutritious. But it was delicious. And cheap.

Every moment was a moment spent exploring. Not an ounce of it was routine or rote.

We stumbled onto shrines hidden away in the crevices of our little neighbourhood.

We learned to fend off the NHK guy who collected TV tax door-to-door (we didn't have a TV).

And, on one sweltering Thursday morning, I figured out that you definitely shouldn't assume chemists open early, lest you want to wait for an hour in the heat with dizzying cramps to buy your desperately needed ibuprofen.

*Traveller's Tips*

# Summer Survival Tips

1. *Deodorant.* Do not trust the forums. You won't find Western-grade antiperspirant no matter how many times you search the cosmetics shelves in Loft. If you have good sense (and you're used to Western deodorant) stock up before you leave.

2. *A hanky!* Have I driven home about the fact that the summer is sweaty, yet? Brow-pattingly sweaty. Neck wipingly sweaty. You can find something cute from Daiso or any other hundred-yen shop.

3. *Cool wipes.* The convenience stores and chemists in Japan sell menthol wipes that make your skin tingly and cold. 'Gatsby' is a popular brand you probably won't miss.

4. *The entire ice cream section of your local konbini.* I loved the watermelon shaped ice blocks with their little chocolate imitation seeds, the matcha vanilla swirl cones, and the little tubs of lemonade ice that came with a slice of lemon on top.

5. *Air Conditioning.* Open windows. A momentary visit to a shopping mall. What's important is taking opportunities to escape the relentless humidity. I spent our first few days in Tōkyō with mild heat exhaustion. Don't overexert yourself if you're from a dry, cool place and are yet to acclimatise.

*Life in Tōkyō*

The summer wore on while I worked on my assignments and waited to hear back about my interview. Late summer is *hanabi* (firework) season. People often dress up in *yukata*—similar to *kimono*, but thinner and worn in the summer—and sit on picnic rugs to watch the fireworks. There are loads of *hanabi* around Tōkyō, and we even watched some from our window.

I especially love the Sumidagawa Fireworks Festival. This one is held in late July, near Asakusa in eastern Tōkyō. It's incredibly crowded (no space for picnic rugs here) but it's worth the few hours' wait to line up and waddle through the streets with the roughly 999,998 other people. Wandering over the bridge and watching the absolutely enormous fireworks bloom and burst in every direction is one of the most beautiful things I've seen in my life.

*Where to Go*

# *Ikebukuro*

## 池袋

Living in Nishidai meant the more popular and busy city of Ikebukuro was only twenty minutes and ¥200 south on the Tōbu Tōjō Line. Our own neighbourhood was very quiet, and so we spent a lot of time in Ikebukuro amongst the bustling foot-traffic and skyscrapers.

Ikebukuro is an unassuming and comfortable city, popular particularly with people who live just outside of Tōkyō Prefecture. Here, we felt a little bit more anonymous. We weren't the local *gaijin* (foreigners) who stood out. Among the crowds, we looked like any other momentary tourists.

Ikebukuro Station is the second busiest train station in the world: second, only, to Shinjuku. And almost every time we went to Ikebukuro, it rained. The irony of this is that we were always on our way to Sunshine City, a multistorey shopping mall at the bottom of a 240-metre skyscraper, filled with restaurants, shops and fun things to do. It's still my favourite place to go in Ikebukuro.

*Traveller's Tips*

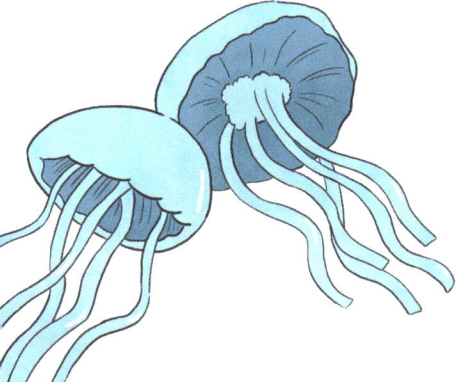

# What to Do in Sunshine City

1. *Go shopping!* Pretty much every piece of clothing I bought while I lived in Japan was from Honeys in the Alta section of Sunshine City. The designs are cute and super affordable.

2. *Check out the amusements.* You can choose from Konica Minolta Planetarium, The Ancient Orient Museum, Sunshine Aquarium and Namjatown (a kid-friendly theme park with carnival-style games).

3. *Get ¥100 sushi from Kura Sushi.* This chain is all over Japan, but we love going to the Sunshine City one. For every fifth plate you put down the chute, you have a chance to win a cute novelty toy.

4. *Watch a performance at the fountain (level B1)!* There are often shows from up-and-coming idol groups, which is an interesting phenomenon if you've never seen anything idol before.

! *Traveller's Tips*

At the end of our first month, I received an email to let me know I had landed that internship!

I couldn't believe how perfect it was: a paid opportunity that I could easily fit around my post grad study.

It took two train transfers, three lines and over an hour to reach the studio each day. Slowly, the costs added up. It was ¥1,160 per day just for transport, which is a lot for someone with no income. But I had received a paid opportunity! With an artist! In Tōkyō!!

After I finished work, Tyler and I would wander around Shinjuku and Shibuya. We loved them both, in all of their difference. Shinjuku for its glittery glass and gleaming lights, a city within a city of relentless movement. Shibuya for its quirky backstreets, busy crossings and unpolished but somewhat youthful atmosphere.

We'd come home late after a long train ride, stroll through our sleepy neighbourhood trilling with relentless orchestral cicadas, and slam on the AC; we had decided, in the end, that this was one of the comforts we were willing to pay for despite our lack of income and the high price of the electricity bill.

But, now that I had my paid internship, I knew we would be okay. The money would soon roll in, I was sure.

We finally acclimatised to the humidity. And, bit by bit, we slowly sunk into a new version of normality.

*Life in Tōkyō*

Don't accidentally sit in the priority seats. And make sure you give up your seat if someone else needs it more than you.

pregnancy badge

Be mindful of your headphone volume so you don't disturb other passengers, don't make phone calls, and make sure to speak quietly if you're with people.

Don't eat on the train. This rule changes for *Shinkansen* (bullet trains).

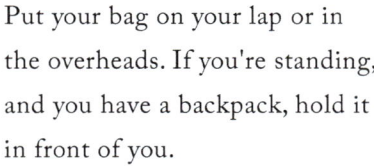

# Train Etiquette

Put your bag on your lap or in the overheads. If you're standing, and you have a backpack, hold it in front of you.

Line up neatly beside the train doors, let all the other passengers get off before you get on, and don't push.

*Where to Go*

# *Shinjuku*
## 新宿

In Shinjuku, you'll find enormous skyscrapers, throngs of people walking swiftly in business clothes, buskers, blaring neon, and a range of tourist attractions like the famous Godzilla head poking out from the Shinjuku Tōhō Building, the Samurai Museum and the free observation deck at the Tōkyō Metropolitan Government Building.

Shinjuku is also home to Kabukichō: the only part of Tōkyō that's usually labelled 'unsafe'. This area is normally only a problem for drunk tourists who are easily conned. I like the area closer to Shinjuku Station. There are quirky and affordable fashion stores above the station. Despite the bustle, the streets are clean, and I find the blues and silvers of the skyscrapers pretty.

During August, I spent a lot of time here running errands for my internship: collecting stationery, ordering prints and buying supplies.

*Traveller's Tips*

# My Favourite Art & Stationery Shops

1. *Sekaido, Shinjuku* – a five-storey, art lover's paradise. The third floor alone is dedicated to paint and traditional art supplies, with a focus on tools for *manga*. If you're into traditional art or comics, you cannot miss this one. Honestly, I could spend a lifetime in this store.

2. *Tokyu Hands, Shibuya* – sells a brilliant range of stationery, craft supplies, interesting knick-knacks, novelty goods and homewares. Their selection of washi tapes is absolutely phenomenal.

3. *Loft, Shibuya* – similar to Tokyu Hands, although with a different selection. The range of stickers, notebooks and journals here is amazing, and so are the post cards. In addition to cute stationery, you can also get cosmetics and interesting gadgets.

4. *Daiso, Harajuku* – any hundred-yen shop is going to offer a great selection of cute, cheap stationery. But I love the Daiso on Takeshita Street (when it's not busy). If you're looking for simple stationery, cheap *origami* paper or fun little souvenirs, Daiso is great.

5. *Muji, Shibuya* – head here for minimalistic notebooks, pencil cases and stationery. They make some nice, cheap pens. This Muji is huge and even has a café in it as well!

*Where to Go*

# *Shibuya*

## 渋谷

If you take the Yamanote Line seven minutes south from Shinjuku, you'll hit Shibuya: Tōkyō's hub for youth culture and fashion. Every TV show about Japan contains at least one clip of the Shibuya Scramble Crossing, one of the world's busiest crossings.

Here, you'll also find the thin pedestrian streets of Shibuya Center-Gai, which is home to both a fiercely popular, week-long Halloween street party in October and, probably, half of Tōkyō's rodent population.

I love Shibuya, though. We spent most of our time here looking at music in Tower Records, perusing the enchanting three storey Disney Store and window shopping at Shibuya 109. For ¥1,800, you can get tickets to Shibuya Sky: a 360° open air observation deck which offers astounding views of Shibuya Crossing and the greater city.

*Life in Tōkyō*

Bit by bit, we began exploring the area around Shibuya. To the south was Ebisu and Daikanyama, both lovely but too luxurious for us. North/north-east was of course Shinjuku, one of Tōkyō's business districts. Further east was Roppongi: a foreigner hotspot known for its clubs. We gravitated west, and fell in love with the residential backstreets of Shibuya Ward: the greater suburb of Shibuya beyond the busy crossings and bustling crowds.

One thing I love about Tōkyō is that, in between snippets of skyscrapers and mayhem, there are winding, sleepy suburbs that muffle the chaos beyond.

Within these snippets, you'll find stout apartment blocks and modern, detached houses, tiny shops with sprawling pot plants, community vegetable gardens, and the staff of local day-care facilities carting around yellow-hatted children in wheeling trolleys.

The more time we spent in the suburbs around Shibuya, the more we realised that this was the side of Tōkyō we loved. We started to look for an apartment closer, with less creepy crawlies and mould.

It would cost more, we knew, but we were losing so much money to train fares; this was money we would save if we could walk more. And if we were lucky, we hoped, we might even stumble across a place with an indoor washing machine.

*Where to Go*

# *Harajuku*
# 原宿

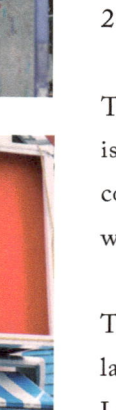

Nestled between Shinjuku and Shibuya is Harajuku. This bright, colourful tourist spot is considered the birthplace of *kawaii* and Lolita fashion. From Shibuya, it's only a 15-minute walk or 2-minute train journey.

The main strip, Takeshita Street, is lined with bold fashion stores, cosmetics shops and places selling wacky sweets.

The culture here has shifted in the last few decades, with many iconic Lolita stores and independent retailers closing to make way for bigger chains.

The old Harajuku Station (pictured) has now been knocked down: one of many infrastructure projects preparing for the 2020 Tōkyō Olympics.

However, the area is bright and lively, and remains one of my favourite places to visit. It gets extremely busy with tourists, but there's plenty of fun things to do around Harajuku.

# What To Do in Harajuku

1. *Go shopping on Takeshita Street.* There are loads of quirky shops selling new and second-hand clothes. I like the clothing chains, WEGO and Ingni. *Tip:* Takeshita Street is quite thin and can become really crowded with tourists, so aim to go on a weekday if you can.

2. *Get crêpes!* This is the most iconic Takeshita Street food, so you can't miss it. There are lots of crêpe stores on Takeshita Street; my favourite filling is caramel, brownie and vanilla ice cream.

3. *Stock up on snacks and novelties at Daiso.* We always grab a few boxes of green tea biscuits, packets of patterned chopsticks or novelty candies as souvenirs for our loved ones.

4. *Visit Meiji-jingu Shrine.* This stunning Shinto shrine is located just beside Harajuku Station. If you see the huge wooden *torii* gate over the path, you'll know you've found the right place. Here you can also buy *omamori* (amulets) for good health, success in your studies and more, or pick out your *omikuji* (paper fortune).

5. *Grab konbini food and have a picnic in Yoyogi Park.* This is my favourite park in Tōkyō. It's absolutely huge, and always lively with people playing instruments or participating in sports with their friends. I love the clever, cawing crows, the open space and the adorable dog run.

*Life in Tōkyō*

In August, an apartment popped up in a leafy suburb in western Shibuya Ward. It was quite a bit more expensive than our current place, although utilities and internet were included in the rent, and we'd already calculated that we would save a significant amount in train fares.

We had savings. But money concerns were starting to weigh on us again. Though I'd been working at my internship for some weeks, I was still yet to be paid. But I was sure we would be fine; I had been told the money would come in soon.

We pored over the pictures. The apartment seemed like a dream. New, clean and gloriously free of mould. It had a lofted space for two *futon* that reminded me of a tree house, a futuristic Japanese toilet, and a shower that would perfectly dispense water at 42 degrees Celsius at the touch of a button.

We fell in love with that tiny, 21-square-foot apartment the very second we saw it.

Within a day of sending off the email inquiry, we had submitted the deposit. Just two weeks later, we moved. We stayed in that beautiful, tiny apartment for the rest of the time we lived in Tōkyō.

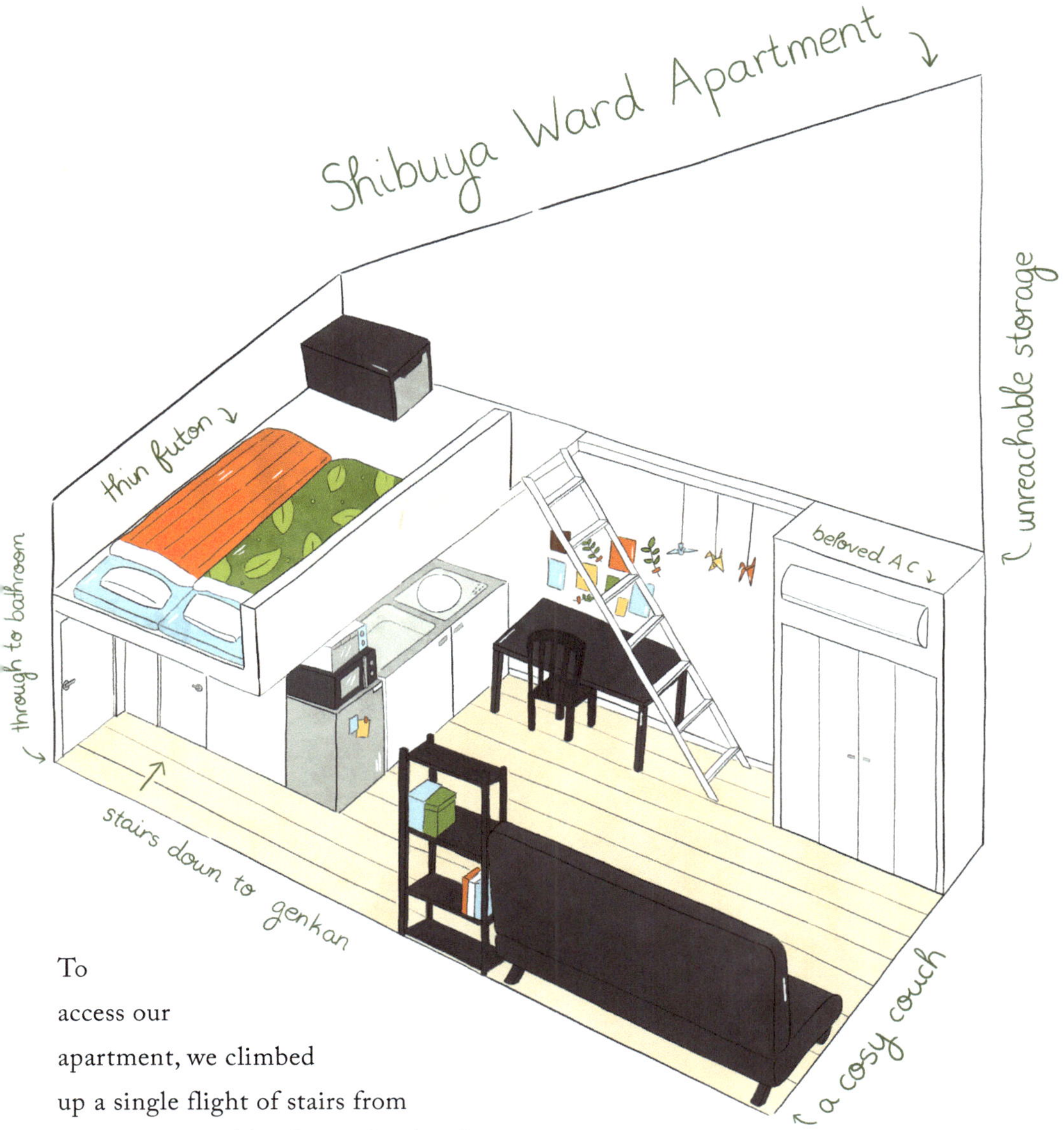

*Life in Tōkyō*

## Shibuya Ward Apartment

*thin futon* ↙
*unreachable storage* ↘
*through to bathroom* ↙
*stairs down to genkan* ↗
*beloved AC* ↙
*a cosy couch* ↙

To access our apartment, we climbed up a single flight of stairs from the street level. The (thankfully) indoor washing machine was located in the bathroom beside the toilet and shower.

It smelled clean, and the walls were soft beige, covered in a textured material you could stick pins in if you weren't scared of losing your deposit. We decorated with posters and paper cranes, and felt at home right away.

 *Life in Tōkyō*

It was almost September and I still hadn't been paid. I found the prospect of confronting my employer deeply uncomfortable and so, ignoring the real problem, I decided to get creative. I found an online magazine targeting female expats called *Savvy Tokyo*. It had an ad on the front page calling out for submissions, and it paid! Thinking I would get turned down, I pitched a mildly ambitious article idea. To my surprise, it was quickly accepted.

Why ambitious? I had offered to visit and review six health food stores across west Tōkyō, knowing full well that I wasn't able to justify paying the pricey train fare to get to these places. But the pitch was accepted and so, with my old Canon camera in hand, I laced up my sneakers and trekked from one side of west Tōkyō to the other and back again.

Over the course of two days, I walked over 25 kilometres.

At the health food stores, I analysed the organic produce available, the offering for vegans, the access from the nearest train station, and I even scrutinised affordability by comparing how much a 400g jar of coconut oil cost at each.

Exhausted, feet covered in blisters, I got home after the second day and started typing up my article. I came out of it with my first ever paid piece of writing: '6 Convenient and Well-Stocked Tōkyō Health Food Stores'. *Note:* the sixth health food store on the list, Lima in Shinjuku, has since sadly closed.

*Traveller's Tips*

# Tōkyō Health Food Stores

1. *F&F - Hiroo*
   This one is directly across from Hiroo Station, making it easy and accessible. It has lots of baked goods and *bentō* (lunch boxes).

2. *Gaia - Shibuya*
   A smaller, local business with an impressive fresh produce section.

3. *Natural House - Aoyama*
   The biggest health food store on this list! It has a large organic produce section and a wide variety of goods. It was also notably cheaper than all the other health food stores listed.

4. *Natural Mart - Hiroo*
   Smaller than the others, but with a nice selection of organic tea.

5. *Waseda - Shinjuku*
   Medium sized, the priciest listed, specialising in natural medicines.

33

*Where to Go*

# Omotesandō
## 表参道

A short walk south-east from Harajuku is the trendy shopping district of Omotesandō. The main shopping strip is lined with huge zelkova trees that are lit up with fairy lights in the winter. If your favourite things in the world are quirky, designer fashion, trendy cafés, and a lovely weekend farmers' market, then this is definitely the suburb for you.

My favourite place to go, however, is the Starbucks on top of Tokyu Plaza Omotesandō Harajuku. There's a stunning view from the balcony. And, true, I've never actually bought anything from the Starbucks here, but the balcony is a wonderful place to hangout—especially while the sun's setting!

Omotesandō remains one of my favourite areas in Tōkyō: a beautiful, leafy place to wander around and window shop.

One cloudy Saturday, I decided to visit here and finally try out one of the trendy cafés I was always peering into. One of my goals was to start vlogging my daily life in Japan and, back in Australia, I had saved up for a new camera. However, because of my lack of income, I ended up using those savings to pay for rent.

*Life in Tōkyō*

In the end, because of the internship, I was never able to replace my old, faulty camera.

However, I decided to become more creative and resilient with it instead. And so, I went to Urth Caffe and bought one of the cheapest menu items—a deliciously fragrant African Tea Latte—worked on another script for my Master's, and filmed a video for my YouTube channel titled: 'A Morning in Omotesandō'.

I felt like an imposter in that lovely café surrounded by designer stores and glamorous young women. ¥580, the price of the latte, was a lot of money to me.

But it was the first proper vlog I filmed while living in Tōkyō, and I'm proud that I made the decision to sharpen my skills with the tools I had, rather than lament our bad luck and make nothing at all.

I spent a lot of time running errands: going to packaging and stationery shops, picking up prints, and managing receipts. I kept on with that internship for longer than I should have.

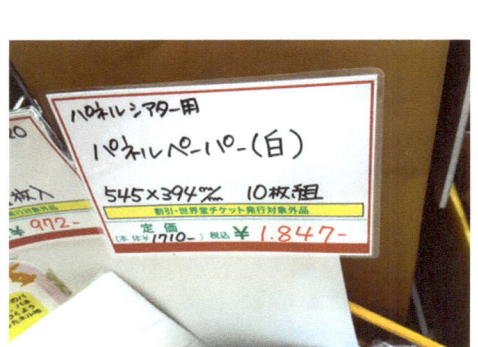

One day, I was alone, coming back from the print shop in Shinjuku. I noticed a man in his twenties in the reflection of a shop window who looked like he might be following me. I went into three separate *konbini*, pretending to browse for a few minutes in each, just to be sure I'd lost him. But, twenty minutes later, almost on the other side of Shinjuku, I looked behind me and there he was.

I was flooded with fear. I couldn't call my boyfriend. I tried to get away. I was walking so quickly it was almost an all-out run. Suddenly, the man sped up and touched me on the shoulder. I jumped half a foot in the air.

He'd asked me a question. In shaking Japanese, I said: *I don't understand you*. He shrugged. He walked away. And I was left, paralysed.

Something snapped in me. I was furious at feeling powerless. Furious that I couldn't afford a phone plan because I was too timid to demand to be paid. I was followed three times while I lived in Tōkyō. This was the second incident and, on this day, I decided I'd had enough. The third time I was followed, I didn't run. I turned around and firmly told the man to leave me alone. For whatever reason, maybe I just got lucky: I was never followed again.

*Life in Tōkyō*

A few days later, I sat in a meeting with the artist, sipping iced tea I couldn't afford. In one sweeping crash, I realised how stupid I had been. I waited until I was walking home before I broke down. It was pouring with rain as I walked, and I would have found that funny if I wasn't so worried, embarrassed and sad.

I passed our neighbour's garden, the rain dripping from the leaves like little tear drops. My umbrella broke in the wind, and whatever resolve I had left broke with it. I was almost sobbing when I opened our door. It was a long night of decision making. I cried a lot. I called home. Tyler made me spaghetti.

The next day, I arrived at my internship and I finally asked the hard questions I should have asked from the beginning. And, when no answers came, I packed up my things and walked out.

I never got the money for the weeks of work I did, but standing up for myself that day made me feel powerful in a way I've never felt before. Because of that one confrontation, I became a stronger and more resilient person. For that, I'm incredibly grateful.

our neighbour's garden

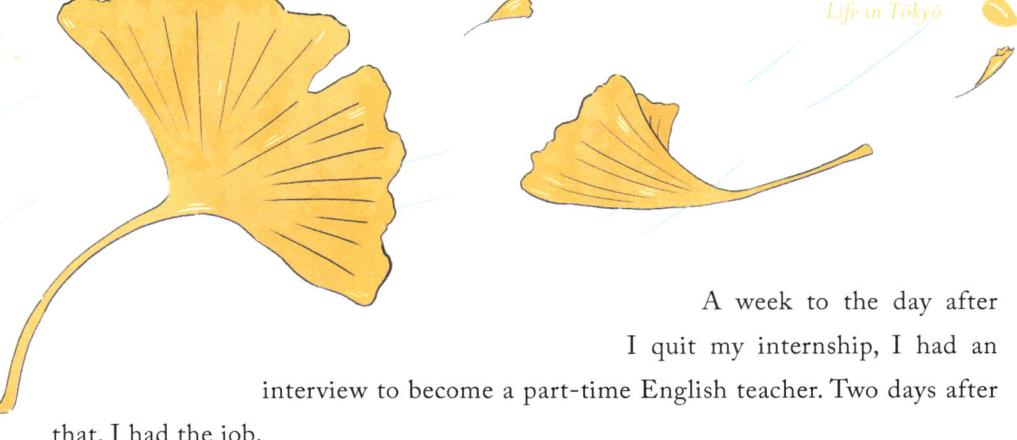

*Life in Tōkyō*

A week to the day after I quit my internship, I had an interview to become a part-time English teacher. Two days after that, I had the job.

The heat and humidity lingered throughout September. There were weeks of grey with no rain. My job interview was the day after a typhoon: the first piece of blue sky I'd seen in ages. Typhoons, the interviewer explained to me, 'suck out' all of the clouds. 'There's always a blue sky after a typhoon', he'd said. With the return of the sunshine, I felt happy and hopeful.

I was to be a *juku* (cram school) teacher who went out to different schools around Tōkyō to teach children aged 3–12 full immersion English. A *juku* is an after-school school or a weekend school for kids. These are incredibly common in Japan—most of the time, kids will have one or two subjects that they study an additional hour per week. In my case, this was English.

The kids called me Christy-*sensei*. I sung them nursery rhymes and we watched children's shows from the 80s and 90s. I read storybooks to them. I taught the younger ones letters and sounds. I taught the older ones about the anatomy of bumble bees and how earthquakes work. They delivered me acorns from their pockets, and were charming, cheeky and surprisingly well behaved. For a person who had initially dreaded the idea of teaching, I absolutely adored my job.

Training to become a teacher was surprisingly laid back. I spent a week with four other expats learning about the practise of full immersion teaching, memorising information about phonetics, and performing pretend lessons. We were each critiqued on what kind of words we used and how we held ourselves. The supervisor told us that the most important thing was to be relaxed: if the kids were having fun, they'd learn what they'd need to.

The Anatomy of a Juku Classroom

A week after my training finished, I found myself in a small classroom in an elementary school in Nakano. The room had the comforting, musty smell of old wood. I had a class of three eight-year-olds and had already forgotten my script by the time I took my shoes off and placed them in the cubby beside the door.

But my supervisor had been right: the kids responded more to my demeanour than the specific content of what I was saying. If I smiled, generally, they smiled. I turned on the interactive TV and began my first lesson.

*Life in Tōkyō*

Christy-Sensei

Being a teacher carried with it a performativity I hadn't expected.

Suddenly, I spent many hours per week speaking with a strange hybrid accent that was mostly Australian but blended in the hard 'r' sounds of an American accent—I was teaching American English, and if I didn't annunciate certain words like 'sister' with a hard 'r' at the end, the kids wouldn't understand what I was saying.

I used this accent so much at work, I found myself accidentally pronouncing words with the hard 'r' sound at home.

I had to dress the most formally out of any job I've ever had. My hair and makeup were exceptionally neat. I had to make sure my tattoo was always hidden by long sleeved shirts. I still wore black nail polish, but if I did my students would point at my fingers and yell, *'Kowai!'*, which means, 'Scary.'

I had a lot of funny accidents: like the time I wrote my entire lesson plan on a white board with permanent marker by mistake, or the rainy Friday I walked the whole way across my classroom in shoes and, realising I hadn't taken them off, almost jumped out of them in fright (thankfully none of my students saw).

But I got the hang of it. Soon I was marking homework with circles instead of ticks, and drawing the much coveted *hanamaru* (flower circle) symbol on all my students' work when they handed it in.

I think this symbol means 'full marks'; I gave it to all of them regardless.

*Life in Tōkyō*

I quickly settled into work, first picking up sporadic relief lessons here and there, and eventually building a consistent schedule.

Mostly, I taught two or three lessons per evening, a few nights a week. By the end of September, I was lucky enough to nab the holy grail: a full, reoccurring Saturday. It was at a tiny, dual-classroom school in a shopping mall, over an hour away in Kanagawa Prefecture. I caught the 7:47 am train there, and wouldn't get home until 8 or 9 pm. But with 7 lessons, that one day of work became half my weekly income.

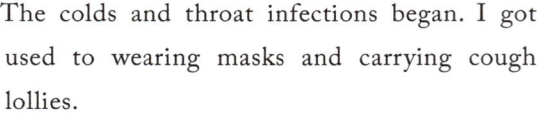

I quickly realised that children are always sniffly, and that they don't cover their mouths when they sneeze or when they're trying to learn how to say the letter 'f' with a comical mix of enthusiasm and aggression.

The colds and throat infections began. I got used to wearing masks and carrying cough lollies.

Slowly, I noticed how living in Tōkyō was rubbing off on me. Here, everyone put effort into their appearance. I stopped wearing yoga pants outside and started to wear presentable clothes, even if I was just going to the supermarket. I never went to work without makeup on—the opposite of what I'd done as a university student working in retail.

I was always a little enamoured by the floods of glamourous women trotting through Shinjuku Station, wearing heels and elaborate half up-half down hairstyles. I loved how effeminate and flamboyant they were for, what seemed to me, no particular reason. Just everyday life.

*Life in Tōkyō*

We made a lot of spaghetti as well as noodle dishes with carrots, potatoes and tofu. The carrots were smaller in Japan, and less sweet, but they were cheap so we ate plenty.

For breakfast, I made banana pancakes every day. We finally found peanut butter in a local international store called Kaldi after trying the abomination known as 'peanut cream' which they sold at our supermarket (peanut cream is a repulsive peanut flavoured jelly). I fell in love with instant *negi soba* (spring onion noodles) and grew used to life without an oven.

Often, we ate dinner out. My teaching assistants—who were generally bilingual middle-aged mothers working part-time—always asked me if I cooked at home. Lots of young professionals don't in Tōkyō. Because of the cost of rice and fresh vegetables, it's often cheaper in Japan to eat at chain restaurants or to get *konbini* food than it is to cook for yourself.

The weather cooled. The cicadas quietened. The sun came out. And as we settled into autumn, we finally learned the most important phrase for ordering food in Japanese: お持ち帰りできますか (omochikaeri dekimasu ka), *'can we please have this takeaway?'*

*Where to Go*

# Kichijōji

## 吉祥寺

My teacher training had taken place in Kichijōji, a popular suburb just west of central Tōkyō. From Shinjuku, it's only 15 minutes on the Chuō line.

Kichijōji is an excellent weekend destination; it's ideal for a sunny Saturday, when you want to visit somewhere peaceful but vibrant. There are trees everywhere, which add to the leafy, bright atmosphere. The vibe here is laid back and welcoming, and Kichijōji is consistently voted as the Kanto Region's most desirable place to live. It's also home to tonnes of cute vintage stores, as well as cafés and restaurants stretching along the backstreets and through Sun Road and Nakamichi-dori.

My favourite part is Inokashira Park, with its sweet little swan boats and its great pluming trees that cascade over the lake. Every day of my training, I grabbed cold rolls and orange juice from the *konbini*, and sat on a bench amongst the foliage and chirping birds, eating and looking out over the lake.

Next to Kichijōji Station

Inokashira Park

*Where to Go*

If you're ever visiting Kichijōji, don't miss out on picking up some *taiyaki* from Kurikoan. *Taiyaki* is a traditional Japanese dessert. It's like a crispy, warm pancake, but shaped like a fish and stuffed with filling. It's firm on the outside, oozy and steaming hot on the inside and is, in my own opinion, the best dessert for the colder months.

*Taiyaki →*

Kurikoan is near the northern side of Kichijōji Station. They sell traditional *taiyaki* flavours like red bean and vanilla custard, but also have an eclectic range of interesting and seasonal flavours too. Sweet potato is popular in the autumn, plus they also have hazelnut, matcha, chocolate and more.

*Tip:* in Japan, it's considered impolite to walk around while eating! You can either stand next to the stall to eat your *taiyaki* or, if you'd like, pop over to Inokashira Park and eat there—it's only a 5 minute stroll away.

It's quite difficult to find bins when you're out and about in Tōkyō. After the Sarin Gas Attacks of 1995, many bins were removed. Sometimes, you can find them in public parks or *konbini*, but keep in mind when you're outside, you may need to bring your rubbish back to your hotel or apartment with you.

*Where to Go*

# *Mitaka*

## 三鷹

Mitaka is only one stop further west than Kichijōji. It's a little bit less leafy, but it's still peaceful and pretty.

This neighbourhood isn't generally known as a tourist destination.

It is, however, a place I always come back to when I visit Tōkyō because it's home to one of my favourite places on this earth: the Studio Ghibli Museum.

If you take the south exit from Mitaka Station and follow the adorable signs along Gotenyama-dori, you'll eventually stumble onto the museum. If walking isn't your thing, there's also a bus you can take from Mitaka Station straight to the museum. You can buy your bus ticket at the station from the vending machine at bus stop No. 9. Otherwise, directly from the station, it's just a fifteen-minute walk.

The actual studio for Studio Ghibli is located a couple stops from here as well. Though, the fact that its address has recently been taken off Google Maps would heavily imply that they don't want tourists to visit by mistake. Or at all.

*Where to Go*

# *Ghibli Museum*

## 三鷹の森ジブリ美術館

Studio Ghibli is the award-winning animation studio responsible for cinematic masterpieces such as *My Neighbour Totoro* (1988), *Spirited Away* (2001) and *Howl's Moving Castle* (2004). Five of the ten highest-grossing *anime* films of all time were produced by Studio Ghibli.

The studio's films—particularly those by lead director, Hayao Miyazaki—are known for their beautiful animation, their painterly and bucolic backgrounds, their enthralling depictions of magic and the fantastic, their bold, young and often female protagonists, and, finally, their mature themes of environmentalism, resilience and hope.

Designed by Hayao Miyazaki, himself, the museum was completed in 2001. The building was inspired by European architecture, with iron spiral staircases and dark wooden fixtures, stained glass windows, balconies and dead ends designed to encourage exploration. In designing the museum, Miyazaki wanted to create 'a building where the breeze and sunlight can freely flow through', leaving the visitor more enriched than when they entered.

## Where to Go

Even if you've only seen one or two Studio Ghibli films, you have to visit this museum. It is a must-see for anyone who is interested in art or animation of any kind. Even the exceptional attention to detail in the design of the building, itself, is an immersive creative masterpiece.

Every corner of the Studio Ghibli Museum is utterly magical. So much work has gone into crafting a space that's just as idyllic and bewitching as any Miyazaki movie.

My favourite part of the museum is the rooms that show the original paintings from the films. One of these rooms contains a desk littered with paints, papers, books and teacups, as if the artist has only just stepped away. There's something otherworldly about this museum. I always leave feeling thoroughly inspired and desperately wanting to draw.

Tickets are only ¥1,000 if you're a resident in Japan, and that includes a ticket to an exclusive short film in the adorable Saturn Theatre. The theatre is located in the museum's basement, with a ceiling painted deep blue and adorned with clouds. You can experience the whole museum in a couple hours—but those are hours you will spend truly enchanted.

*Traveller's Tips*

# Ghibli Tips

1. Organise your tickets through the Ghibli website before you come to Japan. You can't buy tickets at the museum and, if you're purchasing in Japan, the process can be cumbersome. I've watched so many heartbroken tourists turned away at the doors.

2. While there is a daily cap on ticket sales and staggered entry, the museum becomes busiest just after lunch time. If you want to avoid crowds, it's best to go early or later in the day.

3. Be prepared to wait an hour or two for the café. The food is fine. The latte art is beautiful. But if a long wait is going to in any way inhibit your enjoyment of the rest of the museum, skip it. There's a cute hot dog and ice cream stand beside the café if you feel hungry.

4. If you want a prettier walk to the museum, get off at Kichijōji Station instead of Mitaka, and walk through Inokashira Park (the museum is located on the park's edge).

5. Don't forget: you're not allowed to take photos inside the museum. But, there are a tonne of lovely photo spots outside the building, beside the café, and on the rooftop garden, where they have a 16-foot statue of the robot from *Castle in the Sky*.

*Where to Go*

# *Jimbōchō*

## 神保町

In October, the research for my second article took me to the eastern side of Tōkyō. This time, I could afford the train, and I spent the day wandering around Tōkyō's historic and dreamy second-hand book district: Jimbōchō.

Here you'll find thousands of small, thin, yellowing books stacked in piles or peeping from wooden cases. There are bookstores outside, covered up at closing with heavy curtains. Everywhere you look, there are books and books and books.

Jimbōchō is home to around 200 bookshops, as well as Tōkyō's Literature Preservation Society, publishing houses, universities and plenty of *kissaten* (older tea shops), such as Sabouru: an eccentric and retro café in the heart of Jimbōchō. If you're looking for antique books, or if you just want to lose yourself among the dusty shelves of times past, then this neighbourhood is for you.

*Where to Go*

Naturally, Tōkyō's book district has an intriguing history.

Jimbōchō is named after Nagaharu Jimbō, a *samurai* from the 17th Century.

The town was mostly destroyed in 1913 by a huge fire. Afterwards, the scholar Shigeo Iwanami opened a bookstore; this later grew into Iwanami Shoten publishing house, which was responsible for publishing notable Japanese literature such as Natsume Sōseki's *Kokoro*. The area slowly rebuilt, becoming popular with students and booksellers, and eventually turning into the Jimbōchō of today.

The headquarters for Shueisha is also here: the company responsible for producing the *manga* magazine 'Weekly Shōnen Jump'. Without this magazine, we wouldn't have *One Piece*, *Dragon Ball*, *My Hero Academia* or *Naruto*.

Jimbōchō isn't a tourist destination. So, you'll mostly find books in Japanese.

However, some stores do have foreign literature sections. For books in English or other European languages, look for this kanji: 洋書. Pronounced *Yōsho*, it means 'foreign' or 'Western literature'.

 *Traveller's Tips*

# Jimbōchō Bookshops

1.
*The Isseido Booksellers:* 一誠堂書店
1-17 Kanda Jimbōchō, Chiyoda
My favourite of the book shops on this list. It's close to Jimbōchō Station, has two storeys and is home to a beautiful range of antique books in English on the second floor.

2.
*Kitazawa Bookstore:* 北沢書店
2-5 Kanda Jimbōchō, Chiyoda
Lots of books in English about the humanities and social sciences. This bookstore also has a wide range of illustrated books and books about history and linguistics.

3.
*Komiyama Bookstore:* 小宮山書店
1-7 Kanda Jimbōchō, Chiyoda
If you like contemporary art and photography, this will be a great bookstore for you. There's plenty of books here on design, fashion, culture and history.

4.
*Books Sanseidō:* 三省堂書店
1-1 Kanda Jimbōchō, Chiyoda
Here you'll find a lot of Japanese language books. The English section is small, but the bookstore, itself, is enormous.

*Where to Go*

Jimbōchō is a wonderful place to find antique books.

For bibliophiles with a bountiful budget, this suburb will be your paradise.

Do be warned, though: the antique English books are normally really expensive. When I was there, I found a copy of *Mrs Dalloway* for ¥7,000.

Safe to say, when I noticed the small, handwritten price tag, I gently put the book back and slowly moved away.

If you're looking for books that are old and interesting, and budget isn't a concern, Jimbōchō is for you. Otherwise, pop to page 70 for my favourite book shops in Tōkyō—all of those places have affordable books in English!

*Life in Tōkyō*

# Halloween

One of my favourite parts of my job was teaching seasonal classes. In late October, I ran structured, English-language-themed Halloween parties for my students. We did monster bingo and made spooky crafts. At one party, one of the teaching assistants organised for us to do pretend Trick-or-treating up and down the shopping mall that our school was located in.

So, there I was, at this mall an hour out of Tōkyō, in a small-ish town, wearing an enormous witch's hat, holding a huge box of candy and leading twenty children of various ages unintelligibly shrieking 'HAPPY HALLOWEEN!!' at the top of their lungs, while the elderly shoppers around us stared.

I loved that teaching gave me the ability to be silly and have fun. We played a lot of games, and I spent many of the lessons laughing.

There were frustrating moments when my students would misbehave or wouldn't listen, but I never felt anxious with the children in the same way I do when speaking to adults. Kids say what they're thinking. Even if it's harsh.

Like the time my student pointed to a blonde, 40-year-old on the TV and said, 'Hey! Look! It's Christy-*sensei*!'

*Life in Tōkyō*

green tea KitKats ↑

hard-boiled milky candies →

← corn-flavoured, long, puffed-up chip which is definitely for kids...

Ramune (fizzy candies) ↓

# Halloween Candy

(AKA my favourite konbini treats all year round)

Choco Pie ↘

white chocolate with biscuity bits ↘

*Where to Go*

# Tōkyō Disneyland
# 東京ディズニーランド

October was the month where work really picked up for me. In a period of two weeks, I had just one day off. It was almost Tyler's birthday and we had saved to do something nice. So, at the Shibuya Disney store, we bought our tickets to Tōkyō Disneyland for the day before Halloween.

Now, I should be clear: I love Disneyland with every ounce of my being.

But despite being at the happiest place on earth, I was horribly sick the day we had planned to go. The constant colds and sore throats that had begun with my teaching career were persisting. I looked at a number of forums: for many expats who teach small children, this experience of constant illness is apparently quite normal.

I had pretty bad throat infections the whole time I taught English. This was well before the world shifted and isolating when sick was normal. I couldn't afford to take time off work, so I didn't.

I became used to soldiering on: I sang to the kids through a half-lost voice, and I hoarded the packets of tissues that got handed out at train stations with advertisements on them.

So, on my only day off, I put on a mask, downed some (weak) ibuprofen from the chemist, and we headed off to Disneyland.

Shibuya Disney Store

# Disneyland vs DisneySea

One of the cool things about going to Disney in Japan is that you have the choice between two different parks.

Disneyland is the traditional Disney park with iconic rides like 'Splash Mountain' and 'It's a Small World'. It has a castle in the middle and is the older of the two. DisneySea, however, is an ocean-themed park right beside Disneyland. Instead of a castle, DisneySea has a volcano and, instead of a parade, there's a water show on the harbour.

If you're coming to Tōkyō, and you enjoy Disney, it's absolutely worth going to both. However, you can't travel easily between the two parks; ideally, if you want to visit both, you'll need two separate tickets and two separate days.

Disneyland is better for nostalgia-factor and tends to sell out faster because it's more popular in general. But, in my opinion, DisneySea has much better rides.

*Tip:* 'Journey to the Center of the Earth' is my favourite ride, but the line is always really long. Make sure you download the Tōkyō Disney Resort App to grab FASTPASS tickets to the busy rides. These express entry tickets are free!

! *Traveller's Tips*

# My 10 Favourite Disney Rides

1. *Journey to the Center of the Earth - DisneySea*

2. *Tower of Terror - DisneySea*

3. *Toy Story Mania! - DisneySea*

4. *Raging Spirits - DisneySea*

5. *Splash Mountain - Disneyland*

6. *Indiana Jones: Temple of the Crystal Skull - DisneySea*

7. *Space Mountain - Disneyland*

8. *Haunted Mansion (Nightmare Before Christmas) - Disneyland*

9. *Big Thunder Mountain - Disneyland*

10. *Peter Pan's Flight - Disneyland*

*Where to Go*

*mochi →*

My favourite two foods from Disney are the curry-flavoured popcorn from the Arabian Coast in DiseySea and the strawberry, chocolate and custard flavoured Toy Story *mochi* from Tomorrowland in Disneyland.

Bonus points to the *mochi*: the Japanese name is リトルグリーンまん or 'Little Green Man'. 'Man' means 'bun' in Japanese, so this is a play on words. Puns are funnier when you have the added pride of having actually understood the joke in a different language.

Disneyland and DiseySea have differing strengths, so I always visit both. I wear sneakers so that I can walk all day. I am highly strategic with my FASTPASSES. We arrive at 10 am and leave at 10 pm, and love every moment of it.

There are no Disney parks in Australia. I never thought I would be a person who loved Disneyland as much as I do. But, I visited on that first trip when I was 19, and now I'm obsessed. When we went the day before Halloween, we stayed late. October had been a stressful month so I wanted to enjoy every second of this lovely, luxurious day at Disneyland.

There was a laser show instead of the usual ending parade. My throat burned with the fury of a thousand exploding suns, so on the way home we bought some soothing throat spray from Tōkyō Station.

*magic throat spray ↓*

With 40,000+ steps walked in total, I pretty much collapsed into that thin, roll-away *futon* up in our tiny loft bedroom. I fell straight to sleep, my heart so incredibly full.

*Where to Go*

# Mount Takao

## 高尾山

The autumn colours properly hit Tōkyō in November, and the best place to go see them is just outside the city. Mt Takao is about an hour west from Shinjuku Station along the Keiō Line. It's not a particularly difficult hike, but the first twenty minutes or so is the most challenging part. For people who want to avoid the slightly steep incline at the foot of the mountain, there's a chair lift that can take you part of the way up.

Near the base of the mountain, there's a cute shopping street plus the Takao 599 Museum, which is named after the height of the mountain. The museum is free and celebrates the natural environment, particularly the flora and fauna native to the area around Mt Takao.

Mt Takao is lovely all year round, but during autumn it transforms with stunning red, mauve and yellow foliage. The autumn leaves frame the wooden temples at the top of the mountain beautifully. The cleansing incense wafting from the temples adds to the cosy atmosphere. You might even spot some lazy temple cats wandering up the stone steps and exploring the mountain.

*Where to Go*

Once you make it past the halfway point, you can find little shops selling *dango*.

*Dango* is a traditional Japanese snack made from beaten glutinous rice, which is rolled into balls, pierced with a wooden stick and then cooked.

This type of *dango* is savory. It's warm and firm to bite into, and has a similar consistency to *mochi*. I like *kin goma* (golden sesame) flavour, which is a little salty. It's perfect for a chilly day!

At the very top of the mountain, there's a noodle shop which sells delicious *udon* and *soba*. And, of course, there's also a wonderful view overlooking the trees and mountains beyond.

If you're after a simple, nature-centric day trip out of Tōkyō, Mt Takao is a wonderful choice. Because of the stunning views and all-encompassing foliage, it's also the perfect place to visit on a cosy autumn day.

## Life in Tōkyō

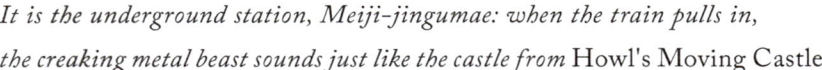

cough lollies

This country tastes like cough lollies and incense—menthol and tradition; old wooden classrooms; cigarette smoke lingering in elevators; hanko *stamping time sheets; character-themed socks against carpet; wet shoes on rainy days.*

It is the underground station, Meiji-jingumae: when the train pulls in, the creaking metal beast sounds just like the castle from Howl's Moving Castle.

It is a whisper, a small bow, a snide eye, an obvious stare. It is hearing 'kinpatsu' muttered by the salary men who pass you. It is struggling with luggage up a flight of stairs, and a stranger running up to help you. It is having a little girl watch you, quizzically, the whole train ride to Sugamo while you pretend not to notice.

Typed into my phone, during the dying days of autumn, on a train from Shinjuku to Sugamo. *Note: kinpatsu* means 'blonde' and *hanko* are personalised stamps used in place of signatures. After every lesson, I had to have someone from the school stamp my time sheet with an official *hanko*.

*Life in Tōkyō*

By the end of autumn, I noticed that I had picked up a number of behaviours from my students and colleagues. My mannerisms had become softer, I spoke with my hands more and my speech became a little slower by default so that people could understand me.

Now, when saying 'no' to my students, I'd gently wave my hand close to my face or chest with my palm facing out, or I would cross my arms to form a big 'x'. And, when I asked my students to 'come here', I beckoned them with my fingers pointed towards the ground (the way we in Australia beckon people, almost as if we're quickly scooping the air towards ourselves, is considered aggressive).

The behavioural differences were fascinating to me; I had students as young as three take off their shoes when they got into the classroom and place them neatly beside the door, or methodically put away their colouring pencils the moment they no longer needed them.

I was struck by the fact that, barely out of toddler-dom, they all seemed neater and more put together than I was.

Around the time I observed this, the ginkgo trees had turned dark yellow in Yoyogi Park. Tōkyō was awash with leaf litter and cold winds that sprinkled dying foliage over the city. I wrote a story about an autumn witch, and filmed a reading of it in the park amongst the crows and golden leaves.

*Life in Tōkyō*

Winter in Tōkyō is bright and brisk. Pastel blue stretches across the sky, and the sun becomes a gentle afterthought, distant and soft.

Where I'm from, the winters are rainy and grey. The days are warmer, but the nights are chilly.

I couldn't believe how different Tōkyō winters would be. It's cold from the second you wake up to the second you go to sleep, and the consistency of the temperature makes it far more comfortable than the winters back home.

When the colder months begin, people drag out humidifiers to combat the dryness. *Oden* (a *dashi* broth based hot pot) and *kairo* (hand-warmer) sales go up at the *konbini*. The cosy seat heaters switch on for the trains. The department stores and shopping centres start blasting their heaters. Those who have *kotatsu* (heated tables) set them up.

December rolled in and it surprised us profoundly that we had been living in Tōkyō for almost six months. My internship debacle felt like a lifetime ago. I finished the first year of my post grad and kept writing articles. Teaching was a little unstable, and money was still a challenge for us, but with the passage of the months, I felt increasingly confident and proud of how far the both of us had already come.

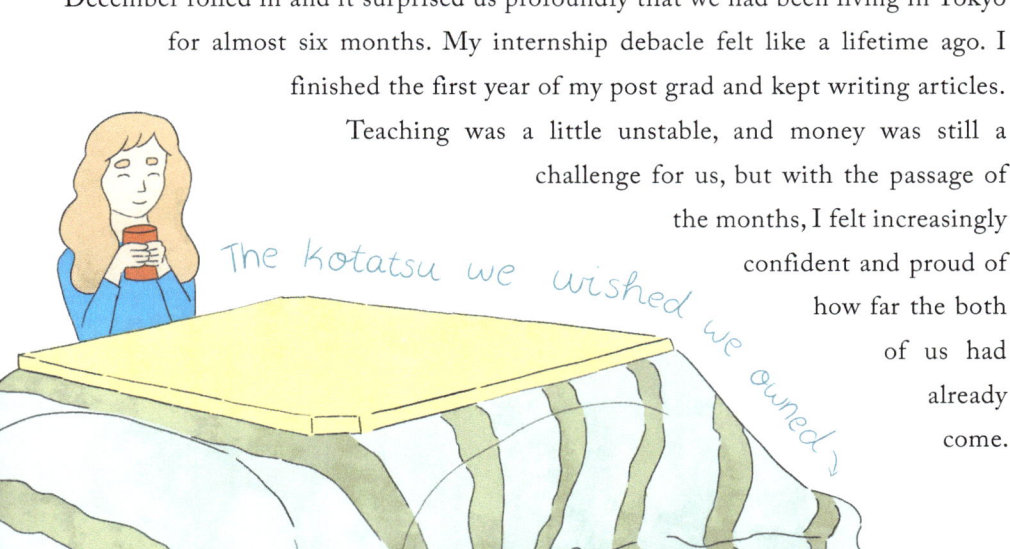

 *Where to Go*

# Ueno Park

上野

On a bristling winter's day, I love exploring museums. Actually, I love a museum trip on any day. But as far as inside attractions go, Tōkyō's museums are great for escaping the cold, and Ueno is full of them.

Located in eastern Tōkyō, Ueno is a popular tourist spot. Take a stroll through Ueno Park—if you go in December, you'll catch the last of the autumn leaves. The park is located beside Ueno Station, and, from there, it's only a short walk to a range of popular museums and galleries.

*Traveller's Tips*

# Top 5 Museums in Tōkyō

1. *The National Museum of Nature and Science - Ueno*
   My favourite museum in Tōkyō! It has beautiful exhibitions and is full of fossils, flora, and elements from the natural world. The museum celebrates technological advancements and the tools and instruments used to preserve and study the world around us.

2. *Tōkyō National Museum - Ueno*
   Opening in 1872, this museum features artworks, antiquities and artefacts from both Japan and greater East Asia. It specialises in art, historical documents and archaeological objects.

3. *Miraikan: National Museum of Emerging Science and Innovation - Odaiba*
   Miraikan celebrates cutting-edge innovation. A must-see for anyone interested in science, technology and the future.

4. *Edo-Tōkyō Museum - Yokoami*
   Experience the historic Edo period (1603-1868) by exploring this museum full of intricate miniatures and life-size dioramas.

5. *teamLab Borderless - Odaiba*
   An immersive, futuristic digital art museum located on Odaiba. The digital pieces move freely in and out of the rooms, and are stunning!

Life in Tōkyō

# Daily Life in Tōkyō

By December, I was teaching roughly 50 kids per week. I worked hard to memorise all of their names and I even remembered the identical twins in my Saturday afternoon class, a pair of loud but sweet eight-year-old boys whom I could only tell apart based on the colours of their glasses. I worked four days per week on average and, on my days off, I studied, wrote articles and stories, and made YouTube videos.

my Nakano classroom

Often, if you ask a child in Japan, 'How are you?', in English, they will respond with the hilariously robotic, monotone, overly formal: 'I-am-fine-thank-you-and-you?'

I had a lot of fun at the beginning of each lesson teaching kids out of this. I would ask, 'How are you?', and say, 'Happy?', with a huge smile. 'Hungry?', and rub my stomach. 'Sad? Angry? Sleepy?'

*Life in Tōkyō*

Once they were comfortable with that question, I'd ask them: 'How old are you?' or 'What's your favourite food?'

I wasn't allowed to speak Japanese in front of them, so my assistants would prod them with hints until they understood and answered.

At the beginning, I'd have to say it slowly, but as my students became more comfortable with my accent I could ask the questions rapidly. One student accidentally told me her favourite food was 'snake' instead of 'snacks'. When I explained the difference, she squealed with laughter. Every lesson from then on, she told me her favourite food was 'snake.'

Watching those kids learn and grow over the months I taught them was one of the most rewarding things I've ever done. The kids I taught were so respectful, so clever and funny, and I was constantly amazed at how rapidly they picked up new information.

By December, we'd become truly settled. We had our favourite local food places. We'd invested in things like kitchen supplies, extra bowls, and a yoga mat. The last dregs of the autumn leaves left Yoyogi Park; the cicadas had long been silenced, but the crows kept on, ominous, echoing, their cawing cutting into the chilly winter air.

Life in Tōkyō

# Tōkyō Bookshop Guide

Even if you can't read Japanese, there are loads of places to find good books in Tōkyō.

The place I spent the most time was Books Kinokuniya in Shinjuku—we often popped in to window shop at night time after I finished work.

We couldn't really afford to buy books, and we also didn't know when we'd leave Japan; the thought of cramming anything else into those already enormous suitcases to take home to Australia filled me with pre-emptive dread.

But despite this, we spent a lot of time perusing bookshops anyway, and wound up with a small handful of favourites which contained a range of affordable and interesting books in English.

*Traveller's Tips*

1. *Books Kinokuniya Tōkyō - Shinjuku*
   Located beside Shinjuku Station, just above Nitori. This bookshop has a wonderful range of books in English (especially books by Japanese authors!) as well as Japanese language textbooks.

2. *Daikanyama T-Site - Daikanyama*
   A beautiful bookstore in upmarket Daikanyama stretching across three modern glass buildings. At night-time, everything is lit up with warm, cosy lights. The range here is absolutely huge, and the store is open late every night.

3. *Book Off - Shinjuku*
   Book Off is a popular second-hand store with many locations. The Shinjuku Book Off, specifically, has a great selection of affordable second-hand books in English. I bought *Alice in Wonderland* and *Bridge to Terabithia* for around ¥400 total.

4. *Tower Records - Shibuya*
   The second floor has a great little book shop! Lots of classics, popular contemporary books and coffee table books.

5. *Animate - Shinjuku*
   A popular chain *manga* store. I've spent a lot of time perusing the *manga* here, and have bought quite a bit in both English and Japanese. Kids' *manga* can make for a fun learning resource if you're starting out with Japanese.

*T-Site* ↙

*Life in Tōkyō*

The six-month mark arrived and we found ourselves waiting in the unfriendly grey chairs of the Tōkyō Regional Immigration Bureau applying for the second phase of our working holiday visa. The Immigration Bureau contained the highest concentration of non-Japanese people we had seen in six months (Japan, an incredibly homogeneous country, is 98% ethnically Japanese. Most of the final 2% are made up of immigrants from North-East Asia).

Despite this building being specifically for foreigners, there was a surprising lack of English. It was stressful, but we found our way. We submitted our paperwork. And, after hours of waiting, our visa applications were complete and we decided to walk to Odaiba: Tōkyō's artificially made island. It was just over an hour from where we were in Shinagawa.

On the way, we saw an *udon* shop. It was old and dwarfed by the skyscrapers it was wedged between. There was such a powerful juxtaposition between this ageing building, and the rapid construction shooting up around it.

There's a Japanese phrase called *Mono no Aware* (物の哀れ) or 'the pathos of things', which relates to an awareness of impermanence. Staring at the building, I was struck by the realisation that this time was so very fleeting. I took a photo of the shop and later painted it in watercolour.

No matter how ephemeral this time in Japan would be, I would always have this picture.

With it, I had frozen a snippet of this rapidly changing city. I would get older. But, in the painting, the *udon* shop would always look the same way as I had seen it, that day in winter, when I was twenty-one years old and living in Tōkyō.

*Life in Tōkyō*

# (Some of) My Favourite Japanese Phrases

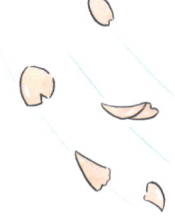

### *Mono no Aware* – 物の哀れ

Many believe this phrase to have become popular in the Edo period (1603-1868), after the scholar Motoori Norinaga used it in his critique of the classical work, *The Tale of Genji*. The phrase expresses an awareness of the ephemerality of life: that all blossoms will fall, all snow will melt and all moments will end. I find it poignant and forlorn in the most beautiful way.

### *Komorebi* – 木漏れ日

There's no direct English translation for *komorebi*—it means 'the light which filters through the leaves'.

### *Shōganai* – しょうがない

*Shōganai* or *shikataganai* translates to 'it can't be helped'. I love the attitude that is attached to this phrase: an acceptance that much of life is out of our control and that's okay.

### *Tsundoku* – 積ん読

To let books pile up in one's home without ever reading them.

### *Shinrin-Yoku* – 森林浴

This translates, literally, to 'forest bath'. Shinrin-Yoku is the practise of spending time in nature for the purposes of improving one's health. The phrase was coined in 1982, and I actually wrote an article about it in *Savvy Tokyo*!

## Where to Go

# Odaiba

お台場

To get to Odaiba, we walked along the Rainbow Bridge. The walk is long and the cars are loud, but it's a unique angle to view the city from. Odaiba is a popular date spot for younger couples—there are a range of malls, museums, concert venues and amusements, such as the *Daikanransha* (Giant Ferris Wheel).

On Odaiba, you'll find both an enormous *Gundam* (robot) statue and a re-creation of the Statue of Liberty overlooking the harbour. The island, and particularly the view of the lit-up Rainbow Bridge before the Tōkyō skyline, is absolutely lovely at sunset.

To celebrate our visa application, we got *katsukare* (pork cutlet curry) and spent the rest of the day wandering the island.

*Traveller's Tips*

# What to Do on Odaiba

1. *Go Shopping at VenusFort*
   One of Odaiba's many shopping malls. VenusFort is particularly cool because of the roof, which is painted to look like a cloudy sky.

2. *Immerse Yourself in Digital Art at teamLab Borderless*
   A breath-taking immersive digital art museum. Tickets are on the pricey end, at ¥3,200 per adult, but the instillations are stunning.

3. *Miraikan: the National Museum of Emerging Science & Innovation*
   Perfect for lovers of technology! Miraikan was created in 2001 by Japan's Science and Technology Agency to create a space for people to learn about the world from a scientific point of view.

4. *Walk Along the Rainbow Bridge*
   Catch the train to Shibaura-futō Station, take the east exit and walk south 500 metres. Once you reach the foot of the bridge, walk down the side street on the left; you'll find an elevator to take you up. If you want a view of Tōkyō Tower, walk along the north side. The south side will give you a view of Tōkyō Skytree. It should take 30-40 minutes to cross.

5. *Visit Donguri*
   Located in VenusFort, this is one of my favourite shops. They have lots of lovely character goods and it's the best place to find Studio Ghibli merch outside the Ghibli Museum.

*Where to Go*

# *Yokohama*

## 横浜

My first advertorial commission arrived! I was asked to write a listicle about outdoor shopping locations in Yokohama, sponsored by one of the malls on the list. I took my camera and set off south. Yokohama, Japan's second largest city after Tōkyō, was only forty minutes away.

Yokohama has a rich migrant history. In 1859, towards the end of the Edo period, Japan's two-hundred-year self-imposed isolation ended, and Yokohama was one of the first ports to open to trade. With the boom of raw silk exports and technology imports, this once sleepy fishing village rapidly grew and became the glittering glass city it is today.

A few weeks after completing that article, I was given some classes to teach at a school beside Yokohama Station. I took the Fukutoshin Line every Wednesday. I never, ever got a seat on that busy afternoon train.

Traveller's Tips

# Places to Visit in Yokohama

1. *Yokohama Red Brick Warehouse*
   Perfect for gift shopping or picking up fun accessories.

2. *Cup Noodle Museum*
   A quirky museum all about cup noodles.

3. *Yokohama Chinatown*
   Japan's biggest Chinatown! Check out the stunning gates and temples, and snag some delicious street food.

4. *Yokohama Minato Mirai*
   Wander around the waterfront and view the Yokohama skyline. The city lights are beautiful at night.

5. *Sankeien Garden*
   A lovely, traditional Japanese garden originally built in 1904.

*Life in Tōkyō*

# Christmas in Japan

Whenever I mention that Christmas is celebrated in Japan, people are often surprised. Unlike in the West, however, it's not a religious or family tradition. There is no public holiday, but you will find many couples booking restaurants and going on dates—in some ways, it's more akin to Valentine's Day.

Sparkling fairy light installations pop up all over the city. Some people decorate and have Christmas parties. Gifts are often exchanged between friends and are sometimes given from parents to children (a number of my students told me they were desperately pining for a Nintendo Switch).

The food traditions, I think, are the most interesting part of Japanese Christmas. On December 25, everyone orders not turkey or ham… but fried chicken. This is all thanks to a clever marketing campaign from KFC back in the 70s. And, interestingly, Christmas is still to this day KFC's busiest sales day of the year. For dessert, people eat 'Christmas Cake', which is sponge cake decorated with whipped cream and strawberries.

One of my favourite things to do during Christmas is visit the Yokohama Christmas Market, held at the Yokohama Red Brick Warehouse. The lights are pretty, and the atmosphere is fun and festive.

*Where to Go*

# *Nakameguro*

## 中目黒

Another great Christmassy spot to go is Nakameguro, specifically around Meguro River. This canal is also called the 'Meguro River Cherry Blossoms Promenade'. It's exceptionally popular in the spring with stunning blossoms hanging over the water. During the winter, however, the bare *sakura* branches are lit up with thousands of tiny fairy lights.

The winter illuminations run from November to early January. Of course, it's incredibly busy around December 25, but it's one of the most festive places to visit in Tōkyō during the holiday season.

We went just before Christmas. Our plan had been to visit the Yoyogi Park Christmas Markets, but we realised after arriving that we'd misread the dates. We did some Googling and found the Nakameguro illuminations. I'm so happy we went there in the end. The canopies of countless fairy lights were enchanting.

*Life in Tōkyō*

On Christmas Eve, we got Christmas cake and dinner from the *konbini*. On Christmas Day, we exchanged presents, video called home and later ended up at our favourite *kaitenzushi (*conveyer belt sushi) place: Kura Sushi.

In Japan, people leave their Christmas decorations up well after December 25. I taught at a school near Sugamo, and the tree beside the station was up until late February. I grew up believing that it's bad luck to leave your decorations up into the New Year and so I found this a little disconcerting.

I didn't mind missing Christmas. The novelty of living in a foreign country still wasn't lost on me. I was in love with the sense of freedom and breathability that came with being far away from the place that I grew up.

I worked the whole way through the Christmas period, teaching seasonal classes through the winter and New Year's holidays. We did festive arts and crafts. My students wrote letters to Santa. I wore a fluffy, red hat. One of my students—the one who now routinely told me her favourite food was snake—realised that my name is similar to the holiday, and started calling me Christmas-*sensei*.

Every time she did, the rest of the kids pealed with laughter. It was one of my favourite Christmases I've had.

# New Year's Eve

The end of the year arrived, my classes went on break, many of the shops shut, and we learned about Japan's New Year's traditions. At Buddhist temples, the bells toll 108 times to remove the 108 types of earthly desires of human beings. People put *Kadomatsu* (bamboo decorations) in front of their doors. Many participate in *Hatsumode*: lining up for hours for the first Buddhist temple or Shinto shrine trip of the new year.

On New Year's Eve, we went to Matsuya for dinner before wandering the cold streets of central Tōkyō. Hundreds of people lined up beside the shrine near our apartment. We headed over to Shibuya, where thousands more stood in the middle of the famous scramble crossing to watch the clock count down.

But the people (particularly the noisy, drunk tourists partying their way through Center Gai) were overwhelming. I think we saw more tourists that night in the packed backstreets of Shibuya than we did even at the Immigration Building in Shinagawa.

We left pretty quickly and wandered back towards Harajuku. We ended up pausing on a street corner, quietly watching the huge screen on the Tower Records building as its clock ticked into the New Year.

*Traveller's Tips*

# Tōkyō's Cheap Chain Restaurants

### Curry House CoCo Ichibanya
*Katsukare* (pork cutlet curry) is my favourite Japanese food, and that's exactly what Coco Curry specialises in. Here you can customise everything from your portions to spice level.

### Matsuya
When we didn't want to cook, we went to Matsuya. This is a chain that serves *gyūdon*: a meal of thin beef and onions in a light sauce on rice. My favourite order is the one that comes with egg and radish, and it's only ¥380.

### Saizeriya
This one sells cheap Italian/Japanese fusion food. The pasta and pizza are great for the price. My favourite, though, is the *doria*: like cheesy pasta bake, but with rice instead of pasta.

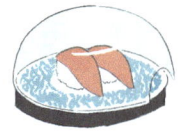

### Kura Sushi
A conveyor belt sushi restaurant where plates are ¥100 each. Every time you slide a fifth plate down the chute beside your booth, you have a chance to win a prize. *Tip*: get there at least an hour before you want to eat, and grab a reservation ticket.

### MOS Burger
My favourite Japanese Western-style fast food chain is MOS Burger. It's cheap, delicious and excellent if you're looking for quick, comforting take-out.

*Life in Tōkyō*

# What We Began to Miss

Every day, I felt grateful that I lived in Tōkyō. But as grateful as I was, living there wasn't easy. In January, I went through a two-week period where culture shock got to me. I hated being stared at all the time. I found the language really tricky. I missed having access to affordable fruits and vegetables. I was sick of being sick.

Eight months later, I would learn that my tonsils were so damaged during this time that they would need to be removed, and that the dizziness and fatigue I felt was actually because of an undiagnosed iron deficiency. But, while we were in Japan, I told myself I was fine. Despite paying the monthly ¥1,361 for health insurance, I was too intimidated to go to the doctors for fear of expensive bills.

One January morning, I lost my IC (metro) card on my way to work not twenty minutes after filling it up. That's what started my two weeks of grumpiness. I felt like our financial situation meant we were missing out on so much: we couldn't afford to go on trips outside of Tōkyō or to try the wacky desserts from Takeshita Street or to go to the bookish capsule hotel I wanted to visit for a video. Without fluency, I knew it would be almost impossible for us to thrive long term.

But, thankfully, this period was short. By mid-January, my delayed culture shock ended, and I felt much better.

*Life in Tōkyō*

It was odd to me that I actually missed things from home like the saturated blue sky or small talk with strangers. And, *of course* finances were difficult: we were students in one of the most expensive cities in the world!

But in the end, what I love the most about Tōkyō isn't the flashy department stores or the outlandish dessert cafés. It's the tiny details: the heavy rain and dense greenery; the jingles played over the speakers at each JR train station; the long-haired dachshund who lived on our street.

Overall, I was proud of our thriftiness. We saved money by walking constantly and by buying *bentō* and fried foods from the grocery store at 9 pm when we knew they'd be on sale. There was, however, an incident where this backfired terribly. One night, we bought a two pack of crumbed fish on sale. We did not translate the *kanji*. We should have translated the *kanji*.

It was late. Exhausted and starving, we quickly prepared dinner: salad, microwave fried rice and the fish. It was small and thin. And, after sitting on our couch, I bit into it. Immediately, I knew something was terribly wrong.

I looked down. The outside was normal but in the belly of the fried fish were hundreds and hundreds of grotesque little eggs. These eggs were now also in my mouth. I yelled. I gagged. I spat it out. My boyfriend pulled out the *kanji* translation app. His fish, so far untouched, still sat on his plate. Unable to control his sniggering, he showed me the translation: pregnant fish.

nightmare fuel ↑
i.e. fish stuffed with eggs

*Life in Tōkyō*

# SNOW!!

The snow came in late January: the second time in my life I'd ever seen it.

When I finished my teaching shift, it was gently falling. I slipped home most of the way in my low, 2L heels (my average Western feet are considered gargantuan at Japanese shoe shops), and rushed to put on sneakers. By the time we got to Yoyogi Park, it was already dark.

The snow had laid itself over the grass like rolled white icing. I couldn't believe that just a few hours prior, the park had been completely bare. It doesn't always snow during the winter in Tōkyō. I had been hopeful, but I hadn't been holding my breath. And so, I cannot describe in words how happy I felt, trudging along the crunchy white frost, umbrella in hand. We ran out into the middle of the park, finding the empty space where people normally play soccer, kicking our feet through the white softness.

I threw myself down into it, and made my first snow angel. My childhood was one of droughts, heatwaves and bushfire action plans. This was so alien and magical to me that I laid in the snow and flapped my arms like a delirious child on Christmas morning.

Life in Tōkyō

It shocked me how much the snow hurt my hands, and how heavy it weighed on our umbrella. By the next morning, some of it had melted. Black ice covered footpaths for weeks. I almost broke my neck several times walking down the hill from our apartment to the train station.

Two days after the trip to Yoyogi Park, we marched to our real estate agent in Nakano to pay our monthly rent, slipping and laughing much of the way. A few weeks later it was gone, melting away into dregs at the sides of the roads and then, eventually, as all things do, altogether fading away to nothing.

*Life in Tōkyō*

Towards the end of winter, we got hooked on Netflix's *Erased*: a live action remake of a *manga* called *Boku Dake ga Inai Machi* ('The Town Where Only I Am Missing').

I went searching for more Netflix J-dramas to cosily binge under the heater.

I was stumped at every turn, however, finding show after show with English titles and descriptions, but no English subtitles. My Japanese was getting better with every month—but I definitely needed the subtitles.

I went looking online, but found no helpful resources. So, I opened my email and sent a pitch off to my editor. I offered to comb through the entirety of Netflix, find all the J-dramas with English subtitles, and rank the best 10.

It took so many hours to search, watch and rank all of the J-dramas. Again, like the health food store article, perhaps I had pitched something a little too ambitious for the ¥9,000 I would be paid in return. But, I was determined. There was a gap in the market, I thought! This was a resource people needed!

As it turns out, I was right. My article, '10 Japanese Dramas To Binge On Netflix' went a little viral. Published February 18, it became the top viewed piece on *Savvy Tokyo* for that year.

*Life in Tōkyō*

# J-Dramas to Binge on Netflix

1. *Erased*
   A *manga* artist, framed for the murder of his mother, is sent back in time 18 years to stop life-threatening incidents before they occur.

2. *Good Morning Call*
   A comedy romance about two high schoolers, Nao and Hisashi, who agree to live together in secret to save money on rent.

3. *Mischievous Kiss (Love in Tōkyō)*
   Almost the exact same premise as *Good Morning Call*, but still light-hearted and surprisingly funny.

4. *Million Yen Women*
   Five mysterious women turn up at the home of novelist Shin Machima, offering him one million yen each per month in rent.

5. *Midnight Diner: Tōkyō Stories*
   A heart-warming drama about good food, advice-giving chefs and the simple importance of healthy human relationships.

6. *Samurai Gourmet*
   A retired salaryman with a *samurai* alter-ego indulges in food.

7. *Underwear (Atelier)*
   A *Devil-Wears-Prada*-esque drama about a young woman trying to make her mark on the lingerie world.

*Life in Tōkyō*

*Shoulders pressed, squashed between suited elbows and backpacks. We are matchsticks: some cindered, some waiting to be. Tourists and salary workers. An old lady with a stooped spine. All in silence. Smartphone screens illuminate the Wednesday afternoon, in-between splashings of sunshine. The hand-holders dangle above. The train throws us lurching back and forth at the mercy of white gloved conductors.*

*The colours of the city smear behind the glass: steel-grey, blue, mottled green. Then, a line of cherry blossoms appear from nowhere. They rise up and greet us, racing us along the tracks, one after the other. They're the colour of strawberry milk, and their skin flakes onto the roads, covering everything in pinky-white. They weren't here last week; they won't be here next.*

*We are the same species: this train, those blossoms. Coming up for air for only a moment, before plunging back into the darkness.*

Taken from my Advanced Poetics Journal, submitted for my Master's course-work, typed on the train from Shinjuku to Yokohama.

*Where to Go*

# *Sangenjaya*

# 三軒茶屋

I visited Sangenjaya for the first time to attend a job interview. In early spring, I started to seriously think about the future. I knew that I couldn't be a post grad student forever; I knew I couldn't teach forever. I had a marketing degree. I figured I should try to put it to use.

So, I applied for a job with a tourism company. I spent two hours in Blue Bottle Coffee, a cute industrial chain café, waiting for an interviewer who would never turn up. The interviewer, it turned out, had mixed up the date. We rescheduled. I was successful in the interview, but I found out that the role paid significantly less than the small amount I made at my teaching job. I politely turned it down.

That was my introduction to the sweet little suburb of Sangenjaya, a neighbourhood known for its restaurants, cafés and bar scene.

# How to Make Egg Toast

Living in Tōkyō made me an expert in eating cheaply. For lunch every day, I either had ¥79 instant ramen or I made some variation of eggs on toast. This recipe was my absolute favourite and I still make it now!

1. Using the back of a spoon, press down the centre of two pieces of bread creating a well in each (this is where the egg will sit).
2. Butter the edges that haven't been pressed down, and then apply Kewpie mayo around the border for flavour and to keep the egg from overflowing.
3. Transfer the bread to a toaster oven or grill, and then crack one egg on each.
4. Season with salt and pepper, and, if you're feeling fancy, a little parsley.
5. Grill for 12 minutes or until the egg is cooked to your liking. Voilà! Egg toast!

*Life in Tōkyō*

# The Week I Turned 22

*Monday, March 5*

I officially started the second year of my post grad! I began research for my thesis, though I wasn't yet sure what angle to take in the area of Fantasy Literature. I spent the day doing course work, developing my Advanced Poetics Journal and studying Japanese. Dinner was an intriguing-looking caramel carbonara from the frozen section of our supermarket (... it was just as delectable as it sounds).

*Tuesday, March 6*

Every morning, I sat at the desk under our ladder and wrote, swapping between freelance articles and creative writing. On Tuesdays, I taught at a school near Odaiba, and so I left for work early in the afternoon. My kids had an English recital for their parents coming up, so we practised their speeches a lot.

*Wednesday, March 7*

After work, I took the train from Yokohama to Shibuya Station, where I met Tyler. We walked to Nitori: a homewares store not dissimilar to Ikea. We'd been cleaning our apartment with a broom and dustpan until this point, and it was time we invested in a proper (albeit cheap) vacuum cleaner. We also got a small fold-away table so that we had somewhere to actually put our food while eating dinner rather than our laps.

## Thursday, March 8

I turned 22. Tyler made choc-chip pancakes, and I unwrapped my birthday presents as the rain bucketed down. Our plans for going to Tōkyō DisneySea had been cancelled by the weather, so we took the train to Sunshine City and went clothes shopping instead. Dinner was spent at our favourite restaurant, Kura Sushi, and we had a dessert of soy ice cream, fried donut and red bean. The next day, Tyler had a job interview: my 22nd birthday ended with a lot of laughter and swearing—I was trying to trim Tyler's hair and accidentally snipped one of the knuckles of my left hand, leaving a triangular cut and, eventually, a little scar that never disappeared.

## Friday, March 9

We went grocery shopping. Tyler had his job interview, and I taught three classes: the first with a sleepy nine-year-old who loved soccer and could never keep his eyes open, the second with an extremely shy six-year-old who never spoke above a whisper and, finally, my group of five seven-year-olds who were noisy and cheeky, and never stopped giggling (or telling me that their favourite food was snake).

## Saturday, March 10

I left home at 7 am; I came home at 8:45 pm. I stood for most of the hour-long train ride there, reading *Peter Pan* on my Kindle. I napped for much of the train ride home. Every Saturday, I taught seven classes of roughly thirty children all together. Lunch was *ebi-onigiri* (prawn rice ball) and cheesy *kare-man* (curry bun), which cost ¥245 total.

## Sunday, March 11

I slept in, watched *The Wind Rises* and worked on a digital painting. I ended my first week as a 22-year-old by finishing up my university homework, reading and starting edits on the video: 'A Week in My Life in Tokyo'.

birthday dessert

*Life in Tōkyō*

Where I grew up, we had almond blossoms: small, white trees, flowering thinly on short branches. When the *sakura* began to bloom in Tōkyō, I realised that they were nothing to the overwhelming majesty of Japanese cherry blossoms.

*Sakura* season explodes at the end of March. The empty arms of gnarled deciduous trees burst, almost overnight, into beautiful pink and white.

In the moonlight, the petals look like tiny ghosts haunting the branches, illuminated by the moon, sprinkling down over the asphalt like confetti. Fairy floss trees. Strawberry milk. Snow, but warm and soft and un-melting in the hands of those swift enough to catch the petals.

One Friday, we stumbled along the Kitazawa River Green Way. Hundreds of breathtaking *sakura* lined the canal. There is something incredibly poetic about these huge trees. Their true selves lay dormant most of the year until spring, when an almost unbelievable metamorphosis occurs. After the *sakura* arrived, I felt like a secret had been shared with me; from then on, I knew which trees were the ones that would bloom and burst in beauty, even after the petals had gone, and they had once again returned to their masks of humdrum green.

*Traveller's Tips*

# Where to See Sakura

1. *Yoyogi Park – Shibuya*
   The open space makes Yoyogi Park a popular choice for *hanami!*

2. *Shinjuku Gyoen Garden – Shinjuku*
   View *sakura* in a peaceful, manicured garden. This is often less crowded than Yoyogi Park, but get there early anyway.

3. *Meguro River – Nakameguro*
   Hundreds of trees overhang on either side of the canal. You can view the blossoms while taking a nice walk.

4. *Aoyama Cemetery – Aoyama*
   A little more forlorn, but absolutely beautiful.

5. *Inokashira Park – Kichijōji*
   Ride the swan boats surrounded by stunning cherry blossoms.

When the *sakura* arrives, so does *hanami* season. *Hanami* is the practice of viewing the cherry blossoms (not to be confused with *hanabi*: firework).

Every year, under the shelter of the sprinkling petals, people gather on picnic blankets with their friends and loved ones, open up their pre-packed *hanami* snacks, and enjoy the beautiful *sakura*.

Local gardens and parks become incredibly crowded, but the atmosphere is a lovely one. The *sakura* only bloom for about two weeks, so it's important to get out and enjoy it while you can.

*Hanami* season perfectly exemplifies one of my favourite things about Japan: people are so enthused to celebrate changes in the seasons and nature.

*Traveller's Tips*

# How to Hanami

1. *Bring a picnic blanket.* And don't forget snack food and drinks. You can pick up loads of fun *sakura*-themed snacks from the *konbini*.

2. *Take off your shoes.* Just like in Japanese homes, people take off their shoes before stepping onto picnic blankets.

3. *Be considerate.* This should go without saying but don't leave your trash. Please don't be loud. Don't take up unnecessary space.

4. *Get there early!* Especially if you want to reserve a good spot on a weekend at a popular location like Yoyogi Park. If you arrive at midday, it's not unlikely that you won't find a spot at all. For company *hanami*, new employees sometimes draw the short straw in being made to wait all day reserving a spot.

5. *Please don't touch the sakura trees!* Be careful of trampling the roots and absolutely don't take cuttings of the branches.

*Where to Go*

# Shimokitazawa

下北沢

Not too far from the Kitazawa River Green Way is Shimokitazawa: a neighbourhood famous for its bohemian vibe, its countless thrift stores and its endless selection of coffee houses.

In the novel, *Moshi Moshi* by Banana Yoshimoto, Shimokitazawa is depicted beautifully as the home of a young woman who has recently lost her father. If you want to feel transported to this neighbourhood, I recommend reading it!

Shimokita is one of Tōkyō's 'hip' neighbourhoods, and it continues to grow in tourist popularity. Despite its busy weekend streets, Shimokita offers something a little different to the fancy shopping strips of Ginza, the neon of Shinjuku and the flamboyant fashion of Harajuku. Like the other main hubs of Tōkyō, it has a unique vibe that can't be found elsewhere.

If you're looking for something more alternative, or if you want to find quirky souvenirs or sustainable resale fashion, Shimokitazawa will be perfect for you.

*Where to Go*

We spent a lot of time in Shimokita perusing the cheap pre-loved clothes. There's an excellent WEGO here, which sells a huge range of bold and interesting fashion, second-hand hoodies with fun prints, and fabulous accessories. I loved window shopping in the vintage stores, which were surprisingly pricier than the non-resale clothing stores.

The backstreets of Shimokitazawa are peaceful and pretty. If you're up for a small stroll, you can wander from the main thoroughfare over to Shirohige's Cream Puff Factory. They sell wonderful little Totoro-style cream puffs in a bunch of different flavours that range from custard to strawberry to chestnut to matcha.

Located near Setagaya-Daita Station, the corner café is nestled amongst the greenery of the neighbourhood, and, to add to the cosy vibe, its building is in a refurbished house. The shop is absolutely adorable, and the cream puffs themselves are delicious. If you love Ghibli, you can't miss it.

The *sakura* disappeared, and we were left with warming days and blooming flowers. My Japanese had improved instrumentally, but it was still a pain point. I often felt self-conscious about it: I wanted so badly to communicate fluently with the people around me.

It comes with being socially anxious. I don't want to stand out, and I often get nervous around others. The difficulty of this peaked on a beautiful spring day. I had a writing deadline. I had to take photos of myself using a translation device for an advertorial article. It was not a good day to have an anxiety attack.

The device was clever and simple: hold down a button, speak English into it and out comes the Japanese needed to communicate with the listener. It could be set to any language, and I could see how tourists would find it useful.

My boyfriend came with me to help. I had a number of university assignments due, and so I was trying to work quickly. We spent the morning in Harajuku and Yoyogi Park, taking photos of the device being used.

In order to show its possible use while ordering food, I lined up at a crêpe stand on Takeshita Street. Tyler took a photo of me speaking into the device, carefully avoiding the faces of the staff or other customers. The experience was a little jarring, but we got the photos we needed. I'd ordered the cheapest crêpe on the menu: the banana custard. We shared it as I planned the last few shots.

*Life in Tōkyō*

For the final photo, I had to get one more picture of the device being used in everyday life. I didn't want to bother a stranger, so I decided to go into a computer store with one of those cute, humanoid robots.

On that sunny spring day, surrounded by flowers and the cheerful blue sky, I was overtired and overwhelmed. The usual stressors were getting to me: being sick, feeling exhausted all the time, finances, my university workload, and the logistics of teaching as many classes per week as I physically could.

As we walked to Shinjuku, my anxiety started to spiral. Because of the sheer weight of everything else, the thing that sent me over ended up being pretty small. It was the final photo: the idea of posing beside a robot like a silly tourist made me so uncomfortable and panicked I was pretty much in tears.

In the end, it was Tyler who helped. We talked until I calmed down and, even though it was my article, he ended up being the one to take the photo of the robot in the electronics store. He was the one who spoke to the persistently inquisitive staff so that I didn't have to. He did everything so that I could get the best photo for my article. I met my deadline entirely because of him.

Navigating a new language and culture can be incredibly difficult, especially if you're socially anxious and are facing a lot of persistent stress. I was lucky beyond belief that he was there with me. As alienated as I often felt, I never once felt alone.

# Where to Go

# Tōkyō Station Area

東京駅

When you tell people you're going to Tōkyō, you could mean one of three things.

Number one, that you're off to Tōkyō Prefecture (東京都, Tōkyō-to). There are 47 total prefectures in Japan, so this is kind of like saying the State of Tōkyō. Number two, that you're heading to one of the 23 special wards of Tōkyō (東京特別区, Tōkyō tokubetsu-ku) which is a smaller region within Tōkyō Prefecture, including cities such as Shibuya or Shinjuku. This area within Tōkyō Prefecture was known as Tōkyō City until 1943. Or, number three, that you're actually going to Tōkyō Station (東京駅, Tōkyō-eki), in Chiyoda's Marunouchi district.

If you're standing in eastern Tōkyō, just outside of Tōkyō Station, checking out the glossy business district of Marunouchi, then you can be in all three at once!

I prefer west Tōkyō—that's where I spent most of my time when I wasn't teaching. To me, the atmosphere is more fun, more vibrant and more laid back in general. However, there are still a wide range of interesting things to do in the eastern section of the city.

Tōkyō Station even has a large underground shopping centre. Yaesu Shopping Mall contains 180 shops, perfect for days when it's bucketing down with rain.

*Traveller's Tips*

# Places to Visit in East Tōkyō

1. *Tōkyō Tower - Minato*
   Catch a stunning view of the city from Tōkyō Tower. Alternatively, you could visit Tōkyō Skytree. It's taller, but more expensive and less iconic. Given a choice, I normally pick Tōkyō Tower.

2. *Tōkyō Imperial Palace - Chiyoda.*
   There are guided tours both in English and Japanese. Don't forget to visit the Imperial Palace East Gardens as well!

3. *Tōkyō Station - Marunouchi*
   Constructed in 1914, the station and plaza are lovely.

4. *Chuo Dori - Ginza*
   Tōkyō's famously expensive designer fashion district!

5. *Tōkyō's Electric Town - Akihabara*
   Tōkyō's *otaku*-culture hub, full of themed cafés and stores selling *anime* paraphernalia. If you're after retro gaming, look for a store called 'Super Potato'! They sell lots of older games and consoles, including Super Nintendos.

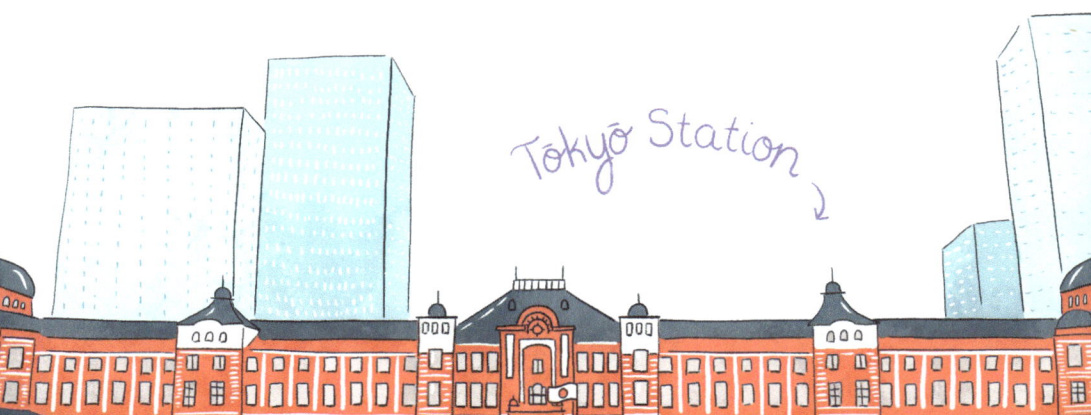

Tōkyō Station

*Where to Go*

# *Asakusa*

## 浅草

A common question often asked by tourists is: 'what is the difference between a shrine and a temple?'

For the most part, shrines are Shinto and temples are Buddhist. These are the two major religions of Japan, with 70% of Japanese people adhering to Shinto practises and 69% of people adhering to Buddhist practises, with many people adopting practices from both. Shrines will often have a large *torii* gate at the entrance, while temples generally have big incense burners. Both will have a station for visitors to wash their hands and mouth before entering.

At a Shinto shrine, the worshipper will bow twice, softly clap their hands twice, and bow again; at a Buddhist temple, the worshipper will wash the cleansing incense smoke over themselves, and, inside the temple, bow and throw a small donation into the box. The most important thing is that visitors are quiet and respectful. Follow the signage and you'll have no issues at all.

I have one favourite shrine and one favourite temple in Tōkyō, both of them popular among tourists.

The shrine is Meiji-jingu, located right next to Harajuku Station. It has a huge wooden *torii* gate, and is surrounded by greenery.

My favourite temple, however, is Sensō-ji.

Sensō-ji Temple is located in Asakusa, surrounded by *kimono* and *yukata* rental shops and old sweets stores. The temple is a bold, vibrant red, and the shopping street leading up to it is always bustling with crowds of people. You can find delicious traditional foods here, and purchase cute souvenirs and knick-knacks for your family or friends.

One of my favourite things to do at a temple or shrine is *omikuji*! Beside Sensō-ji, there's a little spot where you can pay ¥100, shake a tin box, pull out a thin wooden stick with a number on it, and open up one of the draws to find a slip of paper with your *omikuji* or fortune on it for the next year.

The first time, I was super unlucky and got the Bad Fortune. It said: 'every year, your servants will get fewer and you will be alone. Even if you stay in bed for a long time, you'll never get better. It's too dangerous to bring the boat to the shore. Just like a dragon loses its treasure ball, you will lose your hope'.

... thankfully, if you don't like your fortune, you can always tie it up on one of the racks beside the temple or shrine, and leave it behind. That way, the bad luck won't stick with you. If you receive a positive *omikuji*, you can keep it.

*Where to Go*

# Kamakura

## 鎌倉

Spring was coming to its close, and my boyfriend's mum and sister flew to Japan to visit us.

We spent a week showing them around Tōkyō, now playing the role of tourists in this city in which we lived. We showed them our favourite places, and were also able to take them on some fun day trips outside the city. One place we went was Kamakura.

Located just over an hour south from Shinjuku, Kamakura is a picturesque coastal town, popular on weekends.

I have a strangely intense love for train journeys through the Japanese countryside, and the leafy trip down to this seaside town is one of my favourites. I love Kamakura, and strongly recommend visiting.

To avoid the crowds, try visiting during the week, especially if you want to check out the temples. I love walking between the main shopping strip and the *daibutsu* (big Buddha statue) this town is famous for. The backstreets are especially tranquil.

# Top Things To Do in Kamakura

1. *Visit the Daibutsu at Kōtoku-in Temple.*
   Entry to see the famous Great Buddha costs ¥300. Get some green tea ice cream and take your time enjoying the temple grounds.

2. *Climb the steps of Tsurugaoka Hachimangū Shrine.*
   There's a beautiful view of the *torii* gates from the top!

3. *Go postcard shopping at Komachi Street.*
   There are so many interesting little vendors. Perfect for souvenirs!

4. *Get lost in the bamboo forest of Hokokuji Temple.*
   A temple with a small but lovely bamboo grove.

5. *Visit the Kamakura Museum of Literature.*
   Home to both a lovely rose garden and a collection of works by famous Japanese authors such as Sōseki Natsume.

 Where to Go

# Enoshima

## 江ノ島

25 minutes west from Kamakura is Enoshima Island. You can take the retro Enoden train for only ¥260; you'll have a stunning view of the ocean the whole way. If you only have one day, it's absolutely possible to visit Kamakura in the morning and Enoshima Island in the afternoon. However, both towns are very different and to get the most out of them, I think it's better to split them into two separate day trips.

Enoshima Island is a 15-minute walk from Enoshima Station through the town and across a long bridge. From one side of the island to the other, the path is winding. There are lots of small restaurants, a beautiful shrine nestled in the trees and, of course, wonderful spots to look out towards the sea. Watch out for the hawks. There are signs on the island warning visitors about these cheeky food thieves. If you can, aim to reach the peak of the island at sunset. The view is definitely worth the climb!

# Must-See on Enoshima Island

1. *Explore the island in its entirety.*
   Climb all the way to the southern coast; the journey is so lovely.

2. *Visit the Iwaya Caves.*
   Entry is ¥500 to see these mystical caves and old statues.

3. *Have a meal overlooking the ocean.*
   Visit one of the small restaurants high up on the island, and enjoy the view of the sea as you eat.

4. *Visit the observation deck of the Enoshima Sea Candle.*
   There's also a botanical garden. The 360° view is stunning.

5. *Get street food from Benzaiten Nakamise Dori.*
   *Ikayaki* (grilled squid) and *tako senbei* (octopus rice cracker) are popular choices.

*Life in Tōkyō*

Where I'm from, the shift in seasons is mild. Only some of the leaves turn orange in autumn. The winter never feels truly cold. The rain never stays for long. In Tōkyō, however, every month is marked by an intense but beautiful transition. November is known for its vibrant foliage; February for its snow; March and April for their various blossoms. It wasn't until our second summer began that I realised that June's profound natural marker would be the *ajisai* (hydrangeas).

The rainy season begins in early June and lasts until mid-July. With that rain comes the bulbous bright blue and purple heads of *ajisai*. They sprout from the most obscure places, nestled between buildings or at the sides of roads. I never had a favourite flower until I walked along the streets of Shibuya Ward, umbrella in hand, immersed in a sea of hydrangeas.

Another thing I love about the rainy season is *teru teru bōzu* (てるてる坊主). Their name means, literally, 'shine shine monk', and you might recognise them from the 2019 film *Weathering with You* (天気の子, 'Tenki no Ko'). These little ghost dolls are created from white paper or cloth, and were traditionally hung on window frames by superstitious farmers to keep the rain away.

Now, children make them from tissues and ribbon on rainy days when they are stuck inside. If the charm does its job and the rain stops, the *teru teru bōzu* will be given a little face. If not, it'll be thrown away (along with the children's hope to go outside and play).

 *Life in Tōkyō*

With the summer returned the cicadas, humidity and sweat. I loved the heavy rain drops and the flowers that bloomed because of them. We experienced another small typhoon, and I wandered our little neighbourhood, umbrella in hand, watching the rain turn every leaf verdant.

I liked the funny familiarity of the summer humidity—a little less than a year before, it had felt so alien to me. This time round, I didn't get heat exhaustion. It wasn't nearly as uncomfortable as the previous summer. We had acclimatised in more ways than one.

With the return of the heat, though, we realised that our time in Japan was slowly coming to its end.

We kept trying to find long-term solutions. However, without fluency, it's practically impossible to find good, stable jobs that pay more than teaching. Our visas were running out; we weren't flourishing financially and we couldn't see a clear way to live truly comfortable lives as expats.

We began to make plans and, in the meantime, we did our best to enjoy the time we had left.

Where to Go

# Sayama Hills

狭山

Located an hour and twenty minutes west from Shinjuku Station is Sayama Hills: the small town believed to be the real-world setting of the 1988 Studio Ghibli film, *My Neighbour Totoro*. Naturally, the forest located here is known as *Totoro no Mori* (トトロの森 or Totoro's Forest).

The forest, itself, is beautiful. Charming in its isolation, stepping into *Totoro no Mori* immerses you in a pastoral wonderland of greenery, blooming lotuses and crying, cacophonous insects. However, I strongly recommend you don't visit in summer! I emerged with 30 mosquito bites, and a two-week nervousness that I had caught Japanese encephalitis (I was fine).

The day we went was sweltering, and we finished it by heading up to Sayama Lake (also called the Yamaguchi Reservoir). We brought with us a *konbini* picnic of *onigiri* and egg sandwiches, and ate while looking over the open water.

*Life in Tōkyō*

# Summer Reading List

1. *The Wind-Up Bird Chronicle* by Haruki Murakami
2. *Pachinko* by Min Jin Lee
3. *Moshi Moshi* by Banana Yoshimoto
4. *Strange Weather in Tōkyō* by Hiromi Kawakami
5. *The Forest of Wool and Steel* by Natsu Miyashita
6. *Convenience Store Woman* by Sayaka Murata
7. *Sweet Bean Paste* by Durian Sukegawa
8. *The Traveling Cat Chronicles* by Hiro Arikawa
9. *Lonely Castle in the Mirror* by Mizuki Tsujimura
10. *How Do You Live?* by Genzaburō Yoshino

# Shinjuku Gyoen Garden

If you've seen Makoto Shinkai's 2013 film, *Garden of Words* (言の葉の庭, 'Koto no Ha no Niwa'), you would be familiar with Shinjuku Gyoen Garden. Located in the heart of bustling Shinjuku, this ticketed garden carves out a patch of immersive and stunning natural beauty in the centre of Tōkyō. Entry is ¥500. You can see the skyscrapers peeking from the edges of the trees, looming like great silver giants. But, for the most part, once you step into this garden you'll forget you're in the middle of the world's greatest megacity.

Shinjuku Gyoen is home to a Japanese landscape garden, a French garden, an English garden, and a greenhouse. Bring a picnic, a sketch book or something to read. You can even have tea and traditional sweets at Rakuutei Tea House or pop into the Starbucks that recently opened (the architecture of the building blends into the garden surprisingly well).

*Tip:* Not too far from Shinjuku Gyoen is my favourite art supply store in Tōkyō, Sekaido. I love to stock up on supplies before I head to the garden to draw.

# *Odawara*

## 小田原

In late June, I was offered my best commission yet: a two-day, expenses-covered, solo trip to Hakone, in which I would be paid to stay in a luxurious *onsen* (hot spring) hotel, experience a range of tourist activities, and write about them.

I almost jumped out of my chair when I read the email. Aside from cheap day trips, travel outside of Tōkyō wasn't something we'd been able to do. Being *paid* to go on a fancy little holiday felt like a dream. I left home early on a Sunday, battered sneakers on my feet, old camera in my hand, and took the express train an hour south from Shinjuku all the way to Odawara, my first destination.

I was only supposed to stop quickly at Odawara Castle, visit the grounds and the museum inside, look out from the observation deck at the top, take my photos and then head off to Hakone.

However, I was utterly captivated by the stunning hydrangeas surrounding the castle. I wandered the grounds as long as I could before finally, reluctantly, heading back to the train.

# Hakone

## 箱根

After Odawara, I travelled by train and bus along the windy mountains to Hakone. This mountain-side town is one of the prettiest places I've ever seen in my life. It was lush and clean and covered in trees. Lake Ashi sits in the middle; from there, if the weather is clear, it's possible to see a perfect view of Mount Fuji. It wasn't clear the day I went, though: the sky was fogged with soft rain that made the mountains misty and magical.

I ate a small *bentō* lunch from the *konbini*, sitting beside the lake. During peak tourist season, I realised, this place would be packed. I hiked around the lake to see the bright red *torii* gate for Hakone Jinja Shrine—there was a line 50 people long to take a photo at the base of the shrine, looking out to Lake Ashi.

I awkwardly manoeuvred around the waiting tourists and took a photo of the *torii* gate when there was a lull in people posing. Then, I hiked up the hill to the shrine and the museum, and I continued following my itinerary feeling both grateful and tired.

## Where to Go

Afterwards, I got in a taxi and asked the driver to take me up the mountain to the Edo-style tea house on my itinerary. It intimidated me. I had seriously considered walking, but the trek was far and I'd been specifically told to take (and had been given the budget for) a taxi.

As soon as the driver set off, he asked: *doko kara kimashita ka?* 'Where are you from?' The driver spoke slowly, but excitedly. He'd had this conversation many times before. I talked about Australia (*Ōsutoraria*) and the rain (*ame*) and how my country was full of kangaroos (*ippai no kangarū*).

He nodded along warmly and said: *Nihongo jōzu!* 'Your Japanese is great!' The phrase doesn't mean much though; I've been told *Nihongo jōzu* by shop keepers after saying 'arigatō gozaimasu' (*thank you*). But he was a kind man, and I appreciated it.

In the tea house, Amazake Chaya, I ordered the *chikara-mochi* and iced green tea. The wide slabs of *mochi* came in three flavours: *isobe* (soy sauce), *uguisu* (sweet soybean powder) and *kurogoma* (sweet soybean powder mixed with black sesame).

The *mochi* was heavy and warm and delicious.

The floor of the traditional tea house was dirt, and customers sat on logs, staring out through the open doors to the forest. It was chilly and peaceful. I stayed much longer than I needed to, watching the waving arms of the trees, slowly drinking my tea.

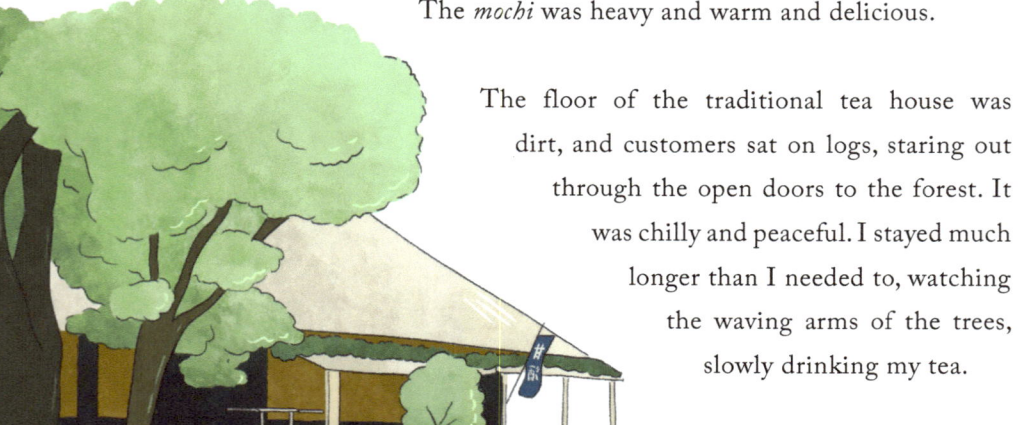

*Where to Go*

I followed along my itinerary, taking the Hakone Sightseeing Cruise across Lake Ashi as the day began to die. I'd been reserved a first-class seat! In a pirate ship! I sat at the front, scribbling in my notebook in between the notes for my article.

*To watch the world float by on a great ship: the steel blue ripples of water, the curves of mountains, their trees like fine hairs. Dimpled. Ruffled. I want to be a pirate of the old world... but we are here and now, and the doors begin to close. The magic ceases. The story ends. I will miss this first-class Hakone pirate ship.*

I stayed in the Odakyu Hakone Lake Hotel and ate at the hotel restaurant. That night, I used an *onsen* for the first time, soaking outside in the volcanic water for over an hour. The cold, night air cooled my face. The water was so mineralised, it almost felt like it had a magnetic buzz. I had spent almost a whole year sleeping on a thin *futon* and so, afterwards, I climbed into my soft bed, my muscles exhausted from carrying my camera and heavy backpack, skin still warm from the *onsen*, and had the best sleep I'd had in months.

The next day I kept exploring amongst the hydrangeas and the mist, before finally taking the train back to Tōkyō.

*Traveller's Tips*

# Things to Do in Hakone

1. *Bathe in a volcanic hot spring.* Onsen are located both in hotels and dedicated establishments like Yunessun (take care to find an *onsen* that allows tattoos if you have them: Yunessun doesn't).

2. *Eat traditional mochi at Amazake Chaya Teahouse.* There's an English menu and the staff are incredibly friendly.

3. *See the billowing smoke at Owakudani.* Who doesn't want to stare into the belly of an active volcano? Try one of the volcano eggs!

4. *Travel across Lake Ashi in a pirate ship.* If the weather is clear, the Sightseeing Cruise is the perfect chance to see Mount Fuji.

5. *Visit Hakone Jinja Shrine.* If you want a selfie with the bright red *torii* gate over-looking the water, make sure you get up early.

6. *Experience the stunning view at Hakone Museum of Art.* To this day, the misty mountain view from the window on the second floor is one of my favourite things I've ever seen in my life.

*Traveller's Tips*

# Onsen How-To

1. *Read the rules carefully.* Even if the *onsen* allows tattoos, it's likely you'll have to cover them up with waterproof bandages. If you have too many to cover, you may need to book a private *onsen*.

2. *Wash before entering.* There will be a section with little stools, showers, soap, shampoo and conditioner. *Onsen* water is supposed to be clean and pure, so you have to enter it already clean.

3. *Yes, you have to be completely naked. Onsen* are separated by sex, if that happens to make you feel more comfortable.

4. *Don't submerge your face or hair in the water.* If you have long hair, you'll want to tie it up after you've washed it.

5. *This goes without saying, but don't stare at people.*

6. *You'll be given a little towel.* You can use it to cover yourself up for modesty. This is generally considered the polite thing to do. Please don't put it in the *onsen* water.

7. *The water is very hot!* To stop yourself from fainting, you can sit on the edge of the bath for a little while to cool down.

# Matsuri Season

From July, *matsuri* season is in full swing across Tōkyō. *Matsuri* simply means 'festival'. Each one is different depending on what that particular *matsuri* celebrates. Most involve a Shinto tradition or ritual, followed by a loud and colourful celebration.

As foreigners unindoctrinated into the culture and customs of Japan's most popular religion, we mostly enjoyed the celebration part: booming drums, bustling crowds, men in white clothing carrying floats, others in traditional dress dancing, and all of them surrounded by red lanterns strung up and swaying in the summer night air.

If you're able to be in Japan during the summer months, make sure you check out at least one *matsuri*. I love the parades and colour. And, although we couldn't understand most of what was going on, I really enjoyed getting to be a part of the bustling crowd and celebration.

Plus, at *matsuri*, street food is cheap, abundant and absolutely delicious!

Life in Tōkyō

# Tanabata

My favourite *matsuri* of all occurs in early July, and it's called *Tanabata* (七夕) or *Hoshi Matsuri* (星祭り, 'Star Festival'). One of my teaching colleagues explained the festival to me on a warm, sunny Saturday. The children were using scissors and coloured paper to make lanterns. Inside the lanterns, and on little strips of paper, they would write their wishes. Of course, we were in class, so the children wrote their wishes in English and I gently helped and made corrections as they did so.

Their wishes were simple. Some of them wished for toys and some of them wished to be musicians or soccer players when they grew up. The eight-year-old identical twins, whom I told apart by the colour of their glasses, both wanted to be police officers. They told me, with brightly glittering eyes, that this was because they both wanted to ride motorcycles.

*Tanabata* occurs on the seventh day of the seventh month. The celebration originally comes from China, deriving from a 2000-year-old Chinese folktale. It was introduced to Japan by Empress Kōken in 755 A.D., and eventually gained widespread popularity during the Edo period (1603-1868).

There are a few versions of the story, but here is the version my colleague told me as we dragged an enormous stalk of bamboo into the classroom to put the children's wishes on: there once was a princess and weaver called Orihime, and a cow herder name Hikoboshi.

Tanabata tree →

*Life in Tōkyō*

The two fell in love, but upon being wed, began to neglect their respective duties. Orihime's father decided to punish the two, and so he separated them, placing each on either side of the Milky Way.

The lovers are able to reunite once per year on the seventh of July.

But, if it rains or is cloudy, the lovers will not be able to see each other across the sky and will, therefore, remain separated for another year.

If the sky is clear, however, and the stars are bright then Orihime and Hikoboshi will be reunited, and everyone's wishes will come true.

I love the folklore behind this particular festival and the fanfare of the colourful paper decorations lining the streets.

One of the most popular places in Tōkyō to celebrate *Tanabata* is at the Shitamachi Tanabata Matsuri. This takes place between Asakusa and Ueno; on the weekend closest to July 7th, Kappabashi Street closes to traffic and pedestrians can enjoy 1.2km of decorations. There's street food and a parade. Plus, if you're walking east, you'll get a view of Tōkyō Skytree peeping out from the swaying decorations and stalks of bamboo.

*Life in Tōkyō*

We wandered slowly around the Shitamachi Tanabata Matsuri, eating street food while I filmed snippets on my camera. Later, I made a video.

Uploaded July 9, the video was titled: 'Why Tokyo?' Here is the transcript.

*We've now been living in Tōkyō for an entire year. The girl of the tiny towns, who didn't know if she'd last three months, has made it twelve.*

*A year of fleeting snippets swallowed up even as I watched them happening into the bottomless recesses of memory.*

*This is now a place that belongs to me.*

*I am twenty-two and I have spent a quarter of my adult life walking beneath these ginkgo leaves.*

*Once, this was just a foreign city, and I did not know its streets better than I know my hometowns', nor did I belong to the crowds, bustling through the* matsuri *and storm clouds.*

*Once, my favourite museum was a strange and obscure building I had not met yet. My favourite park was a green, angular shape on a map unexplored by my worn boots. But then, a visa application, plane tickets, and a question sculpted by the mouths of strangers and friends over and over: why Tōkyō?*

*I would tell them rudimentary things about cleanliness, and safety, that didn't capture how*

*Life in Tōkyō*

*this city feels to a person who has spent a lifetime searching for magic in between the cracks of ordinary objects.*

*I would tell them how, even though it's busy, it is so beautiful; even though it is loud and bright, it holds the most profound silence in between its fingertips.*

*This place has taken a piece of me and will not give it back.*

*I am young. One day, I'll have a house. A dog. A library of books not a row of boxes taped up and stuffed in the back of someone else's wardrobe. One day, adulthood will win. It will take me and tie me down by the arms and legs, but for now, I am free.*

*I threw myself to the wind, and here is where I landed, again and again…*

*I found enchantment in between the scattered pot plants and the umbrellas bobbing along the roads.*

*I found peace in the noise and chaos of a megacity. I found everything.*

*And I will have to leave one day, but I will be back again and again, and every time this city will take more pieces of me, but—willingly—I will give them.*

*I will end up a soul scattered between many countries, but I cannot think of a more joyful existence than sailing the oceans of extraordinary.*

*Life in Tōkyō*

That day when I made Tanabata lanterns with my students was actually one of my last days of being a teacher.

The end of our time in Japan had arrived, and we used up pretty much the last of our savings on the flights home. Although I knew it was a desperate last-ditch effort to stay, I still couldn't find any stable marketing jobs that would give me the financial peace of mind and work visa I needed.

By the end, I was teaching around 14 consistent classes a week. That meant I had to do 14 different goodbyes. I'd been surprisingly stoic for most of them, but when my Saturday class of five-year-olds collectively burst into tears and engulfed me in a sad hug, I lost my composure.

The funniest goodbye was my Friday afternoon group of seven-year-olds. There was an assistant that day who couldn't speak English. As I've mentioned: my being a full-immersion teacher meant I wasn't allowed to speak Japanese in front of the kids. Often, they'd ask me questions in Japanese and I'd nod or answer in English. For some reason, the kids never realised I could speak it.

Whispering, because I didn't want to disrespect the rules, I asked the assistant in Japanese to take a photo of the kids and I together. The kids heard me and gasped, horrified: 'Eeh!? She could speak Japanese the whole time??'

*Life in Tōkyō*

We contacted our real estate agent and gave up our tiny Tōkyō apartment. We called the water company. I cancelled my phone.

In late July, we went to a BiSH concert on Odaiba. And, shortly afterwards, as we walked out into the night surrounded by the sweaty crowd of alt-idol fans, we realised that we had just made the worst decision of our lives.

How could we possibly leave this place we loved so much? Neither of us wanted to go back to the apartment. Going to sleep meant coming a day closer to leaving. We walked all over Tōkyō until the dark sky turned pink.

We spent a few days looking at cheaper apartments, alternative teaching jobs, visas and any possible avenue to make this work. I don't think I've ever felt more lost than I did for those three days, stuck in our apartment, trying to problem solve the impossible. Eventually, once the frenzy of regret had passed, we realised that this horrible sadness and denial was actually grief.

For us, leaving was incredibly difficult because neither of us actually wanted to go.

But, we'd made the decision that we thought was best for us and, eventually, we accepted it.

I began to say goodbye to what had been the best year of my life: the year I turned 22 and became a published writer who lived in Tōkyō.

# The Last Week

Over the course of our last week, we revisited our favourite places: we got *taiyaki* from Kichijōji, we visited Kura Sushi in Ikebukuro, and we walked lap after lap of Yoyogi Park. I spent hours wandering around our leafy little neighbourhood, taking pictures and saying goodbye to it.

The night before we left, we stayed in a cheap hotel in Shinjuku. Our water was off, our electricity gone, and our *futon* rolled away. The next day, we'd hand back our keys.

That night was warm and humid, illuminated by the neon lights of Shinjuku bouncing off the white shirts of salary workers ferrying past us. We got *tonkatsu* (breaded pork) for dinner and, afterwards, our favourite snacks and watermelon ice cream from the *konbini*. We walked back to the neighbourhood that was no longer ours; we said goodbye again to the tiny apartment that was now empty.

On the last day, after dropping off our keys, we lugged our 30kg, broken-wheeled bags onto the train and across the city.

It was terribly hot and uncomfortably reminiscent of the day we arrived.

I couldn't even feel sad. I was too stressed about getting our dodgy luggage onto the plane and which books I'd have to throw away at the airport if we were over the allowed weight limit.

*Life in Tōkyō*

Our plane left at 8:25 pm on August 1.

I sat in that seat a completely different person to the one that had arrived more than a year earlier.

In such a short space of time, I learned and experienced so many things. We had no idea if we'd survive one month, and we made it thirteen.

My year spent within the city of ginkgo leaves changed me irrevocably.

As we flew over the Philippine Sea, I scribbled in my notebook:

*The moon, which I had thought for some amount of time was a light attached to the wing of the plane, is bright orange-yellow. And the ocean, so far below, reflects a fragment of its lustre. That great beast beneath—how many fish, creatures, and sights unseen do we pass over at this moment and do not realise? What universe exists down there that we do not yet know?*

*There is beauty in the tiniest things: a jellyfish, a wildflower pushing up through the concrete, a crow cawing from the Yoyogi Park gate. There exists enchantment in typhoons and sakura and snow. In children's songs. In hydrangea blooms.*

*Severing the light in sponge marks, lifting paint from the coat of inky black, the clouds look like islands, and they make me feel like Wendy fluttering over them. I put my finger on the glass, double pane. The sky and all its possibilities are an exhibit; I could touch it, but I cannot. The plane flies home. And I realise, rather fleetingly, that this is the closest I will ever be to the moon.*

Epilogue

# Life as an Ex-expat

So, what happened after I came back to Australia?

I got a job in marketing, I kept writing travel articles about Japan, and I never quite got over my teacher's need to talk with my hands. I went back to Tōkyō for a holiday right before the pandemic started and visited our old apartment in Shibuya Ward.

I graduated from my post-grad studies. I had my first piece of fiction published. And, eventually, after a lot of hard work and saving, I was able to achieve one of my biggest goals: I quit my full-time marketing job to become self-employed and make YouTube videos and write.

Without my time in Japan, I'm not sure I would ever have had the confidence to do what I've done. That time has rubbed off on me in so many ways: I still sometimes accidentally annunciate the hard 'r' sound when I talk. I still do the small almost-a-bow-but-not-quite head bob when someone in a shop gives me something. And, after eating it almost every single day for a year, I still can't quite stomach the smell of most broth-based instant ramen.

But, most impactfully: I was able to take the leap to become self-employed because living in Tōkyō gave me the confidence that no matter what challenge I'm given, I will find a way to be okay.

*Epilogue*

Living in Tōkyō was a lesson in resilience: in building up the ability to, almost on a daily basis, bounce back from challenges.

Living in a foreign country means constantly learning. It means finding ways to be  comfortable in the arms of relentless discomfort. Every conversation, train ride, or visit to a shopping centre teaches you a little more about culture, both your own and the one you're immersed in.

It gave me more insight into what it's like to be 'the other'—to navigate the persistent unpleasantness of having strangers openly stare at you because of your ethnicity or loudly talk about you while assuming you can't understand them. For this increased understanding, I very thankful.

Moving to Tōkyō at twenty-one is probably the bravest and wisest thing I've ever done. I am an infinitely stronger, more confident person because of it.

I am extremely grateful to every person that I met while living there; I am grateful that because of my country of birth, I was able to get the visa I did; and I am grateful that my primary school made me take Japanese lessons as a five-year-old, kickstarting this life-long interest.

I urge you: if you can, leap outside the bubble of where you grew up. The experiences that allow us to grow the very most as people are often the ones that terrify us. If I, the anxious patron saint of imposter syndrome that I am, can move to the other side of the world without a plan, job or place to live, then you too can take the leap beyond your comfort zone. Go out into the world. Experience the beauty, the diversity, the nuances and enthralling complexity of this planet we get to live on, and the people we're lucky to share it with.

*Epilogue*

Writing this Tōkyō guide and memoir has given me the ability to finally process the amazing thirteen months I spent living in Japan. It has been incredibly cathartic to sit down and go through my notes, photos and vlogs to work out which bits I should and shouldn't include in this little book.

There are plenty of things I omitted simply because there wasn't enough room. A number of restaurants and shops I loved shut down during the pandemic, and so I left them out. I also learned so much about language, culture, people and even myself that I couldn't include concisely in this small guide and memoir.

With this book, I wanted to give a succinct but honest snippet of my experiences.

There was a lot of joy and magic and awe, but there were also a lot of challenges and anxiety. At times, living in Tōkyō was tremendously stressful and difficult, despite how much I loved it and how sad I was to leave.

Tōkyō is a truly enchanting city. No matter how many times I visit, I can't shake my love for it. Whenever I'm not there, all I desperately want is to return. But the world is a funny place, and these things are not always easy.

While I lived in Japan, I spent a lot of time writing articles and resources about the Tōkyō 2020 Olympics. I typed out thousands of words about volunteering and how English speakers could get involved, and wondered where I would be in the world when the games were finally on. I never imagined that I would be writing the postscript of this little guide just weeks after the games finally came to pass, postponed, of course, because of COVID-19.

*Epilogue*

I want to say an enormous thank you to the people who helped me with this guide and memoir.

Firstly, to Sumi, the colleague and friend who explained Tanabata Festival to me: she kindly agreed to Sensitivity Read *A Year in Tōkyō*, and also checked all of the Japanese. Her feedback was exceptionally helpful.

Thank you to Jonnie, Kacy, Bron, Missy and Pippa for their friendship, support and for their help with this project. Thank you to Miranda, Mayra, Mohini and Ruxandra for their wonderful feedback as Beta Readers. Thank you to Mia, my beloved (non-biological) sister, for proofreading the project.

And, finally, to Tyler: my best friend and partner, who not only spent the whole year with me in Japan, but who also read countless iterations of this guide, and whose help and feedback were instrumental in making it as good as it possibly could have been.

I hope you've enjoyed this book. I hope you found it in some way useful or entertaining. Above all, I hope that I was able to capture even a small snippet of the magic of this place where I have now spent so much of my time.

# Tōkyō Itinerary

Here is a simple, seven-day itinerary that you can use to plan your trip!

## Sunday - Arrive in Japan

**Evening:** Travel to Tōkyō from Narita or Haneda Airport. Check into your hotel and grab some dinner; if you get in really late, convenience stores in Japan have surprisingly great dinner options.

*Tip:* for this itinerary, it's best you pick a hotel in Shinjuku.

## Monday - Harajuku, Shibuya & Shinjuku

**Morning:** visit Meiji-jingu Shrine in Harajuku. Get crêpes and go shopping along Takeshita Street. Grab a picnic from a convenience store and eat lunch in Yoyogi Park.

**Afternoon**: Head to Shibuya where you can visit the world's busiest crossing, the Shibuya Scramble, check out Shibuya 109 shopping mall, and catch a stunning view of the city from Shibuya Sky.

**Evening**: Explore Shinjuku at night, visiting the quirky department stores above the station as well as Sekaido, an amazing five-storey art supply shop.

## Tuesday - Ueno, Asakusa & Minato

**Morning:** explore Ueno Park before heading to the National Museum of Nature and Science (science, tech and nature), and Tōkyō National Museum (history and art).

**Afternoon:** get your *omikuji* (paper fortune) at Sensoji-Temple in Asakusa.

**Evening:** visit the iconic Tōkyō Tower in Minato and look out over the city at night.

## Wednesday - Disneyland

**All Day:** take the train to Maihama Station and spend the day at Disneyland!

## Thursday – Daikanyama & Jimbōchō

**Morning:** visit one of the world's most beautiful book shops: Daikanyama T-Site.

**Afternoon:** peruse second-hand books in the city's book district, Jimbōchō.

**Evening:** rest. Tomorrow's a big day, so you might want an early night.

(**Alternative!** If you're more into tech, instead head to Odaiba where you can visit the immersive digital art museum, teamLab Borderless, as well as Miraikan: National Museum of Emerging Science and Innovation.)

## Friday – Kamakura & Enoshima

**Morning:** Travel to Kamakura to visit the Giant Buddha, climb the steps up to Tsurugaoka Hachimangū Shrine and, finally, go shopping along Komachi Street.

**Early Afternoon:** take the Enoden train along the sea to Enoshima.

**Evening:** explore Enoshima Island and watch the sunset from Enoshima Sea Candle.

## Saturday – Kichijōji & Ikebukuro

**Morning**: Take the train to Kichijōji, and walk through Inokashira Park to the Ghibli Museum. After, grab *taiyaki* (fish-shaped pancake) from Kurikoan.

**Afternoon & Evening:** Head to Ikebukuro, and visit Sunshine City: a shopping mall inside a skyscraper. Grab dinner from Kura Sushi (but make sure to get there early to secure a reservation ticket). After, visit the planetarium or aquarium.

## Sunday

**Morning:** After you check out, ask the staff at your hotel if you can leave your bags with them. Then enjoy Shinjuku Gyoen Garden before heading to the airport.

*Note:* one of the very best parts of travelling is taking your time to explore and stumble across tiny snippets of magic. Don't feel the need to follow this itinerary precisely. Every location mentioned here has a wide range of things to see and do: much more than I could fit on two pages. Go gently. Soak in and learn as much as you can. I hope you have an absolutely remarkable time.

# Index

## Neighbourhoods

| | |
|---|---|
| Akihabara | 105 |
| Asakusa | 19, 106-107, 127, 138 |
| Daikanyama | 27, 71, 139 |
| Ebisu | 27 |
| Enoshima | 110-111, 139 |
| Ginza | 100, 105 |
| Hakone | 118-122 |
| Harajuku | 25, 28-29, 34, 82, 102, 107, 138 |
| Hiroo | 33 |
| Ikebukuro | 11, 20, 132, 139 |
| Jimbōchō | 50-53, 139 |
| Kabukichō | 24 |
| Kamakura | 108-110, 139 |
| Kichijōji | 44-45, 49, 97, 132, 139 |
| Mitaka | 46 |
| Nakameguro | 80, 97 |
| Nakano | 40, 87 |
| Nishidai | 11, 12, 20 |
| Odaiba | 67, 72, 74-75, 94, 131, 139 |
| Odawara | 118 |
| Omotesandō | 34-35 |
| Sangenjaya | 92 |
| Sayama / Tokorozawa | 115 |
| Shibuya (City Centre) | 12, 22, 25-28, 56, 71, 82, 94, 97, 138 |
| Shibuya (Ward) | 27, 30-31, 33, 113, 134 |
| Shimokitazawa | 100-101 |
| Shinagawa | 72, 82 |
| Shinjuku | 6-8, 12, 20, 22, 24-27, |

140

| | | | |
|---|---|---|---|
| | | Iwaya Caves | 111 |
| | 33, 36, 42, 70-71, 97, 103, 117, 132, 138-139 | Kitazawa River Green Way | 96, 100 |
| | | Konica Minolta Planetarium | 21 |
| | | Lake Ashi | 119-122 |
| | | Matsuri | 124, 126-129 |
| Sugamo | 62, 81 | | |
| Ueno | 66-67, 127, 138 | Meguro River | 80, 97 |
| | | Meiji-jingu Shrine | 29, 107, 138 |
| Yokohama | 76-78, 94 | | |
| | | Mount Fuji | 119, 122 |

## Sightseeing & Attractions

| | | | |
|---|---|---|---|
| | | Mount Takao | 60-61 |
| Aoyama Cemetery | 97 | Namjatown | 21 |
| Daibutsu / Great Buddha | 108-109 | Odakyu Hakone Lake Hotel | 121 |
| Disneyland | 56-59, 138 | Odawara Castle | 118 |
| | | Onsen | 118, 121-123 |
| DisneySea | 57-59 | | |
| Enoshima Sea Candle | 111, 139 | Owakudani | 122 |
| Godzilla, Tōhō Building | 24 | Rainbow Bridge, Odaiba | 74-75 |
| Hakone Jinja Shrine | 119, 122 | Sankeien Garden | 77 |
| Hakone Sightseeing Cruise | 119, 121-122 | Sayama Lake | 115 |
| | | Sensō-ji Temple | 107 |
| | | Shibuya Crossing | 26, 138 |
| Hokokuji Temple | 109 | Shibuya Sky | 26, 138 |
| Inokashira Park | 44-45, 49, 97, 139 | Shinjuku Gyoen Garden | 97, 117, 139 |
| | | Shinjuku Station | 24, 42, 71 |

| | |
|---|---|
| Shitamachi Tanabata Matsuri | 127 |
| Sumidagawa Fireworks Festival | 19 |
| Sunshine Aquarium | 21 |
| Sunshine City Fountain | 21 |
| Tanabata / Hoshi Matsuri | 126-130 |
| Tōkyō Imperial Palace | 105 |
| Tōkyō Met. Gov. Building | 24 |
| Tōkyō Skytree | 75, 105, 127 |
| Tōkyō Station | 9, 59, 104-105 |
| Tōkyō Tower | 75, 105, 138 |
| Totoro no Mori | 115 |
| Tsurugaoka Hachimangū Shrine | 109, 139 |
| Ueno Park | 66, 138 |
| Yokohama Chinatown | 77 |
| Yokohama Minato Mirai | 77 |
| Yoyogi Park | 29, 63, 69, 80, 86-87, 97, 99, 102, 132-133, 138 |
| Yunessun | 122 |

## *Books*

| | |
|---|---|
| Book Off | 71 |
| Books Kinokuniya Tōkyō | 70-71 |
| Books Sanseidō | 52 |
| Daikanyama T-Site | 71, 139 |
| Kitazawa Bookstore | 52 |
| Komiyama Bookstore | 52 |
| Summer Reading List | 116 |
| The Isseido Booksellers | 52 |

## *Museums*

| | |
|---|---|
| Ancient Orient Museum | 21 |
| Cup Noodle Museum | 77 |
| Edo-Tōkyō Museum | 67 |
| Ghibli Museum | 46-49, 75, 139 |
| Hakone Museum of Art | 122 |
| Kamakura Museum of Literature | 109 |
| Miraikan | 67, 75, 139 |
| Samurai Museum | 24 |
| Takao 599 Museum | 60 |
| teamLab Borderless | 67, 75, 139 |
| The Nat. Mus. of Nature & Science | 67, 138 |
| Tōkyō National Museum | 67, 138 |

## Food

| | |
|---|---|
| Amazake Chaya | 120, 122 |
| Benzaiten Nakamise Dori | 111 |
| Blue Bottle Coffee | 92 |
| Curry House CoCo Ichibanya | 83 |
| F&F | 33 |
| Gaia | 33 |
| Kura Sushi | 21, 81, 83, 95, 132, 139 |
| Kurikoan | 45, 139 |
| Matsuya | 82-83 |
| MOS Burger | 83 |
| Natural House | 33 |
| Natural Mart | 33 |
| Sabouru | 50 |
| Saizeriya | 83 |
| Shirohige's Cream Puff Factory | 101 |
| Starbucks | 34, 117 |
| Urth Caffe (moved to Daikanyama) | 35 |
| Waseda Natural | 33 |

## Shopping

| | |
|---|---|
| Animate | 71 |
| Christmas Market, Yokohama | 78 |
| Daiso | 18, 25, 29 |
| Disney Store | 26, 56 |
| Ingni | 29 |
| Kamakura Komachi Street | 109, 139 |
| Loft | 18, 25 |
| Muji | 25 |
| Nakamichi-dori | 44 |
| Sekaido | 25, 117, 138 |
| Shibuya 109 | 26, 138 |
| Shibuya Center Gai | 26, 82 |
| Sun Road | 44 |
| Sunshine City | 20-21, 139 |
| Super Potato | 105 |
| Takeshita Street | 25, 28-29, 84, 102, 138 |
| Tokyu Hands | 25 |
| Tokyu Plaza Omotesandō Harajuku | 34 |
| Tower Records | 26, 71, 82 |
| VenusFort | 75 |
| WEGO (Harajuku) | 29 |
| WEGO (Shimokitazawa) | 101 |
| Yokohama Red Brick Warehouse | 77-78 |

# About the Author

Christy Anne Jones is a writer, illustrator and video maker from Adelaide, Australia. She has been loosely studying the Japanese language and culture since she was five years old, and has published over 30 travel and culture related articles about Japan. She drinks a lot of green tea and has dedicated her life to searching for magic in between the cracks of ordinary objects.

www.ingramcontent.com/pod-product-compliance
Lightning Source LLC
Chambersburg PA
CBHW041501010526
44107CB00049B/1611